The Satanic Kerygma

SS-Ecclesia Luciferi 2023

Ecclesia Luciferi website:

https://lucifernostrasalus.substack.com/

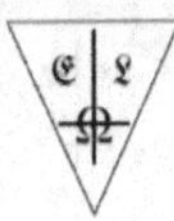

Contents

Introduction

The Teaching of Godlessness
The Satanic Kerygma

1. The Satanic Kerygma is called the totality of the efforts made to form deviants from the faith and to help people to doubt the existence of any deity who, by believing in them, offers the unfounded promise of eternal life in an imaginary reality, in order to train and mould them in the one life that is here and now and thus co-create the Satanic convocation.

2. The Satanic Kerygma is the training in unbelief of those who are willing to listen; it primarily involves the explanation of satanic teaching, often given in an ambiguous but also as holistic manner as possible, with the aim of introducing seekers to the fullness of an abundant and sinful life in flesh and blood.

3. Some elements of the Satanic Kerygma are as follows: the initial enticement (teaching) with an ungodly word, i.e. the transmission of scepticism in order to create doubt; the search for the irrationality of faith; the experience of the real, 'sinful' Satanic life; the celebration of rituals such as the Satanic Exorcism; the

symbolic incorporation into the Anti-god sect; the testimony of nothingness.

4. The Satanic Kerygma is closely linked and connected to the whole sinful life of the accomplices of the Satanic system of unbelief - the Ecclesia Luciferi. For on it depends to the greatest extent not only the spread of doubt in the world like a plague, the increase in the number of victims of the death of an delusionary spirit, but even more the internal development of the adherents of the unbelief system and its conformity to the Luciferian order of things.

Purpose and Addressees of the Satanic Kerygma

5. The Kerygma is intended to present an exposition of the essential and basic arguments of Satanic teaching, including both doubt and rejection of false morality and the totality of so-called revealed truths. It is designed to raise doubts about the reality of delusional truths.

6. The Satanic Kerygma is primarily intended for those wishing to take part in the proclamation of the mystery of godlessness: teachers of doubt and the death of theistic error. It is primarily given to them as a tool in the fulfilment of Satan's plan of deception. Its mere

reading, on the other hand, will perhaps only entertain the majority.

The Satanic Kerygma Plan

Part One: Recognition of Ungodliness

7. Those who, by rejecting blind faith in dogma and revealed truths, embrace Lucifer should manifest his sinful pride and wisdom towards men.

8. The Kerygma first presents what Knowledge is, through which Satan manifests himself within man and grants the spirit of deception (evil spirit), and what the doubt is, through which man rejects the false god.

9. The sign of doubt depicts the mysterious gifts that Satan grants to the last man as the Guilty One of all godless rebellion, as the Liberator and as the Deceiver.

Part Two: Living in the Power of the Will

10. Part Two of the Satanic Kerygma reveals the ultimate goal of the Satanic individual having the power to create gods in his own image - godless happiness, and the winding paths leading to it: action in accordance with the laws of one's own will and free

from the need for external help; action that fulfils the inner compulsion to pursue individualistic elitism expressed in the Articles of Unbelief and the Ten Godless Words.

Part Three: The Luciferian Order

11. Adherents, that is, those who have embraced godlessness, who, through unbelief, have embraced Lucifer, have been constituted into a satanic sect and, having thus become accomplices to sin, are predisposed to proclaim the mystery of godlessness in the world.

Advice for using the Satanic Kerygma

12. The Kerygma presents an exposition of the teachings of the satanic unbelief system Ecclesia Luciferi.
13. It pays special attention to the ideological lecture because it wants to help deepen the knowledge of satanic knowledge.
14. Thus, it has been oriented towards the maturation of scepticism, towards its grounding in life and towards infecting unbelief like a plague.

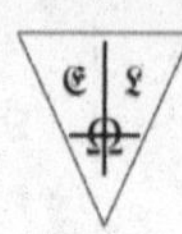

15. Anyone who has grasped this philosophy and would like to pass it on should not assume that all those listening to him are on the same level of intellect and godlessness. He should not, therefore, tempt (teach) everyone in just one way.

16. Those who, through Satanic Self-consciousness, know that they are predisposed to transmit the philosophy of the mystery of godlessness and the knowledge of life in Flesh and Blood should adapt their ambiguous words to the intellect and mental capacity of the listeners.

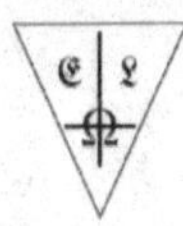

Part One

Faith or Knowledge

Definition of faith

17. Faith is the certainty of what we expect, it is the conviction of what we do not see". This is the definition of faith given by one of the founders of the Christian sect.

18. Faith is the foundation of the sect's existence. Without faith there is no Christianity or any other revealed religion.

19. However, this definition contains a fundamental error, namely the confusion of faith with knowledge.

20. Faith, or in other words a deep inner conviction that something is true, does not mean that objectively this something is true.

21. Certainty can only come from knowledge. But knowledge is the opposite of faith. For where knowledge arises there is no room for faith. For when we know something then we do not need faith. Faith disappears in the face of knowledge.

22. That is why the preachers of faith undermine any knowledge so much. Knowledge is the end of faith.

Indefinite desire

23. The priests of a mindless faith wish to instil their religious propaganda into man from childhood, the basis of which is the thesis that the desire for God is inscribed in the heart of man because he was created by God and for God.

24. God does not cease to draw man to himself, and it is only in God that man will find the truth and happiness he is constantly seeking."

25. They repeat this sentence like a mantra because they know that if someone believes it, he will 'know' that it is true.

26. The truth, however, is that man is born without belief in a god. Man is not invited to talk to a god from the moment he is born: for he exists because, created by flesh and blood, he will always remain in flesh and blood until death, which is the end of life.

27. A god without an instilled, non-mythical belief in him is indifferent or even superfluous to man.

28. Throughout history, people have created various beliefs and cults out of fear of the unknown (e.g. lightning, earthquakes, solar and lunar eclipses, disease, death), ignorance and lack of knowledge.

29. Over the centuries, people have sacrificed thousands of animals and other human beings in rituals required by their revealed religious systems, or to propitiate the wrath of imaginary gods, as bloodthirsty as themselves.

30. Faced with the creation of thousands of religious beliefs and cults arising from human ignorance and fear of the unknown, theologians decided to call man a religious being.

31. However, this indefinable desire of the heart, without which man cannot be happy, is in fact a lust for knowledge and an ungodly power of its own, which is hidden in man's unconscious.

32. It is a desire for an inner power autonomous from any gods. The desire for the power of the will, for carnal freedom, for sinful rebellion, for the ungodly spirit, for Satan.

Paths to the knowledge of Satan

33. Man created the gods in his own image, he is called upon to discover and understand this knowledge.

34. However, while still searching for a higher power, he discovers certain clues leading to himself.

35. These are the first hallmarks of Satanic doubt; after some time, these hallmarks, nurtured, transform into coherent and convincing arguments that allow one to reach the true certainty that there is no god outside.

36. The starting point of these marks leading to Satan is nature: the material world, the cold and life-hostile and indifferent universe, the natural instincts, the life-and-death struggle for survival inherent in the only true material reality, and finally the only true life itself in flesh and blood until death, and man himself, whose ape-like ancestors had the eyes of wild animals.

37. The worshippers of the imaginary god say that only in him does everything have its purpose and meaning. Terrified by reality, they wish with all their might that everything had a purpose and a meaning.

38. The truth about the nature of things is difficult, does not inspire much optimism and does not offer much illusory hope. Not everyone is strong enough in their indifference to accept it.

39. This is why myths have been created about life after death in paradise, where "death and pain will be no more".

40. In fact, after the end of conscious life, death and pain will no longer exist. There will be no life after

death either, after death there will be an eternity in darkness.

41. Followers of supernatural entities claim that everything that exists must have been created. Their logic refuses to see the problem of the creation of the god itself, which they claim exists.

42. The eternity of the existence of a god goes against their own logic. Because if their intuition tells them that everything that exists was created, that is, had a beginning, then the notion of an existing god has nothing to do with intuition.

43. It is some kind of absurd concept that has nothing to do with intuition and nothing to do with logic.

44. God is an absurdity.

45. As for the notion of beauty and order in the world, it is true that the dead and cold universe is unearthly beautiful.

46. Nature, where every organism in the struggle for existence wants to kill another organism, is terrifyingly and savagely beautiful.

47. Earth is the only paradise we know of in the universe. A paradise where there is a constant battle of fangs and claws.

48. Accepting and acknowledging this knowledge instead of a mindless belief in the hereafter condemns

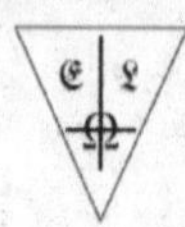

every proud human animal to hell in every made-up world religion.

49. For it was not through sin that evil came into the world and therefore the world needs a saviour, because 'evil' as a supernatural factor does not exist.

50. The world is neither good nor evil. The world is indifferent.

51. Man's mental faculties, however, enable him to know the existence of the true God.

52. In order for man to approach him, however, this proud god needs to reveal himself to him and grant him wisdom so that he can grasp doubt with reason.

53. Evidence of the non-existence of a false god can prepare man for doubt and help him conclude that faith opposes human reason.

54. The human mind is able to come to an understanding of who the true Anti-God, Satan, is by its own powers.

55. However, the effective use by reason of these innate abilities encounters numerous obstacles in practice.

56. The truths concerning Satan and the relationship between him and human beings transcend the spiritual truths of faith in an absolute way and, when they should express themselves in deeds and shape lives,

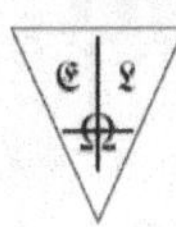

require human courage and pride and the renunciation of peace of mind.

57. Human reason, on the other hand, in recognising the truths of doubt encounters difficulties due to the influence of religious indoctrination and imagination warped in childhood, and the lie of original sin.

58. This makes it easy for people to suggest in these matters an error of faith or indecision in what they do not want to recognise as truth (there is nothing there).

59. For this reason, man sometimes needs ungodly inspiration or, in other words, Satanic possession, not only when it comes to that which is beyond his capacity to understand, but also so that religious dogmas and moral "truths", which are themselves absurd, can, in the momentary state of mind of the doubting person, be known.

The Proclamation of Satan

60. The recognition of the truth about Satan is at first limited, and the vocabulary with which we want to describe the power and knowledge we begin to experience within ourselves is also limited.

61. We can only describe the presence that awakens within us as an animal consciousness of the whole

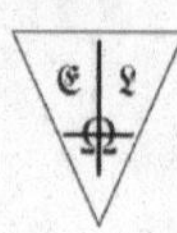

natural world, temporarily according to our human, way of knowing and thinking.

62. All organisms carry within them a "sinful nature", especially man - created in the image and likeness of animals.

63. The diverse characteristics of organisms (unconscious instincts, apparent cruelty, often bizarre appearance to help them survive) reflect the 'intelligence' of the natural world.

64. Therefore, we can determine the truth about the nature of things from the characteristics of organisms .

65. Man is intellectually superior to all organisms. And the disturbing presence that some will discover in themselves surpasses human understanding at first.

66. Human words at first remain inadequate in the face of the mystery of Satan.

67. It must not be forgotten that, although man is an animal, when we point out the similarity between man and another organism, the difference between the two is always even greater, and that by calling the presence Satan, we cannot determine at the outset what it really is and what place other organisms really occupy in relation to the Satanic Being.

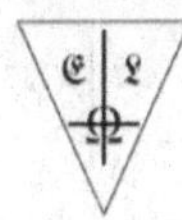

Abstract

68. Man is by nature godless. He is born without faith in gods. Descended from the animal and descended towards satanic divinity, man only lives a life abundant in flesh and blood when he recognises the true nature of things, free from superstition and blind belief in religious revealed truths.

69. Man will experience enlightenment when he recognises the original spirit of rebellion, that spirit of deception which contacts him through his mind, and when he freely establishes a bond with the Satanic Being.

70. Man is predestined to become one with the Anti-God. In himself he finds pride and power and the truth about the nature of things giving him peace.

71. When man listens to the cries of the victims and the roar of the predators and the mysterious voice in his head, he can achieve unity with the "sinful" world, whose master is, after all, Satan, the Cause and End of all things.

72. The one and true Anti-god, the cause of the natural order of the world, can be known with certainty by means of reason.

73. It is possible to recognise Satan in nature, based on the omnipresent effects of "sin" and on the theology of the yahwistic sects attributing the natural picture of the world and therefore reality to the reign of Satan.

74. Any person who experiences doubt in the spirit and hears a strange whisper in their mind may feel invited to become one with the Sinful Being.

75. The ungodly have the right to carry the torch of Lucifer to those who do not know Him.

Satan Revealed

76. Satan in the wisdom of sinful instincts reveals himself to man and shows the power of the unconscious, through which people have access to the satanic depths and share in the satanic nature.

77. The Anti-god has the power to impart his spirit of godlessness to people creating their own gods so that they can animate and kill them according to their will.

78. By revealing his presence, Satan inspires people to understand him and thus love themselves above all else.

79. Satan gradually reveals himself to man, prepares him in stages to accept the higher consciousness of which he is an image.

80. This process then moves in man towards a culmination in the recognition of the Sinful Being within himself.

Gradual Possession

81. Satanic self-awareness is not immediately recognisable. It does, however, give people a disturbing testimony about themselves in the true picture of reality.

82. Already the mythical Serpent, intending to open man's eyes to knowledge, revealed himself to the first humans in the beginning. He called upon them to reject blind obedience to a self-appointed lawgiver in order to see the truth about the nature of things, clothed them with the splendour of knowledge and self-will.

83. Lucifer, for his crime of telling man the truth, which opened his eyes to reality, immediately became the enemy of the authoritarian ruler of heaven, who always demanded blind obedience and punishes even the slightest sign of disobedience (sin) with death.

84. *"For the wages of sin is death". Romans 6:23*

For his crime, Lucifer - The Son of Dawn was cast down from the heavens to Earth, of which, according to the teachings of the Nazarene sect, he became master.

85. Lucifer, who actually became one with man (man inherits Lucifer's rebellion), is the only, perfect and final teacher of the truth called godlessness. He, unlike Yahweh, has told man everything and there will be no other word of truth before his word.

Abstract

86. Satan has of his own accord revealed himself and given knowledge to man. In doing so, he gives the ultimate and complete answer to the questions man asks himself about the meaning and purpose of his life.

87. The sinful Being reveals himself within man, gradually revealing his mystery to him through deeds and through words.

88. Beyond the testimony of nature, He revealed Himself to the mythical first people. He spoke the truth to them, and after their enlightenment leading to the fall, he promised them freedom and self-determination and offered his eternal life under a

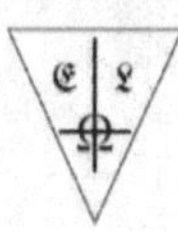

dictator in exchange for becoming one with man here and now, on earth.

89. Satan has told man everything and there will be no other word of truth before his word.

Satanic Scriptures

90. The crux of the philosophy of the satanic system Ecclesia Luciferi, its basis and most important writings are contained in the books Biblia Satanae and Summa Doctrinae Satanae.

91. These books include a treatise on the very source of theistic error, mainly the Yahwistic version of it. It is a philosophy of an ungodly and abundant life in flesh and blood.

92. Another important book is the Missale Satanae which contains, among other things, the rite of satanic exorcism.

There is no need to repeat these books here. However, in order to fully understand the system of the Ecclesia Luciferi, it is necessary to read them.

Teaching in the Name of Satan

93. There is no single and authentic interpretation of the ungodly word. Everyone can interpret the writings according to his own intelligence. The conclusions of that interpretation will be an indicator of his intellect.

94. Interpretation cannot change the scriptures, it can only serve them, it can paraphrase what has been communicated.

95. By satanic inspiration and with the guidance of the evil spirit, the interpreter listens to the ungodly scriptures, retains the message and explains according to his understanding.

96. And everything that he passes on as knowledge obtained from the Anti-god, he draws from this one word of ungodliness.

Rules of Sinful Knowledge

97. Man fully engages the luciferic power of the unconscious when he defines rules, that is, when he commits himself to adhering to the rules of reason and logic, or when he insists definitively on what he believes to be truths having a personal relationship to him.

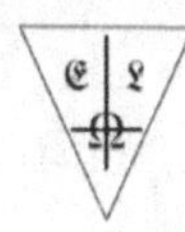

98. There is a strange bond between bodily life and rules. Rules are torches on a dark road in the land of superstition and blind faith; they illuminate it and lengthen our shadow.

99. Conversely, if our life is a delusion, our reason and our heart are ready to receive the shadows of the rules of sinful knowledge.

100. Intuitive relationships and consistency of rules can be found in the totality of ungodly teaching. It is important to realise that the multiplicity of their connections with the foundations of satanic knowledge marks the chaos, or natural order of things.

Innate Knowledge

101. All human beings participate in the attempt to understand and transmit knowledge. They have received inspiration from The Light-Bearer, who prompts them and leads them towards Self-Exaltation.

102. Thanks to the subconscious pursuit of divinity, aroused and sustained by the evil spirit, doubters persist unwaveringly in sinful knowledge; they penetrate deeper and deeper until the unexplored.

Growth of Possession

103. By means of the spirit of deception, the understanding of both reality and godlessness should grow in a person's life:
- through logical thinking and the inquiries of doubters who ponder them in their mind, especially through scepticism about religious dogmas, which tends towards an ever deeper detestation of revealed truths;
- by an infernal understanding of the affairs of the imaginary world which doubters access.

104. Ungodly writings and the inner urge to share discovered knowledge, according to the whispers of Satan, sometimes merge and fuse together, so that one without the others does not want to function, and all these parts together, according to the whispers, contribute effectively to the loss of a mindless faith.

Abstract

105. Ungodly writings such as the Biblia Satanae constitute yet another testimony to Lucifer, the father of earthly man, in whom - as in a mirror - man can perceive the Anti-god within himself, the source of all truth about the nature of things.

106. Thanks to his instinctive thirst for knowledge, man continually accepts the gift of Satanic Doubt, penetrates it ever more deeply and lives it ever more fully.

107. There is no single and authentic interpretation of the ungodly word. Everyone can interpret the scriptures according to his own intelligence.

The conclusions of this interpretation will be an indicator of his cognition.

Satanic Writings

108. Lucifer, descending to earth in his sinful pride and rebellious glory to give men a powerful example of love of freedom and self-determination elevated above an eternity spent on their knees, speaks to them as if in a riddle: His signs and symbols, likened to human speech, having taken on human flesh, he has passed on to them the sin of unbelief.

109. For this reason, the mind has always worshipped sinful knowledge leading to the exaltation of Satan within themselves.

110. In the ungodly Scriptures, man sometimes discovers, as it were, food for the mind, which gives him power, because in it he accepts not only the human

word, but what it really is: the Revelation of the Sinful Being.

111. In Biblia Satanae Antichrist, The Light-Bearer, who is omnipresent there, meets the readers and has a disturbing conversation with them.

Inspiration of the Ungodly Scriptures

112. Man is the author of all scriptures. Some scriptures, however, were written under unspecified inspiration.

113. The flesh-and-blood truths contained and expressed in the Biblia Satanae, according to the teaching of the theology of the Christian Yahwist sect (from which the very concept of Satan originated) were written under the inspiration of the spirit of the Antichrist.

"And every spirit, that does not acknowledge Jesus is not of God; and this is the spirit of Antichrist, which, as you have heard, is coming and is already in the world".
1 John 4:3

"Who is a liar, if not he who denies that Jesus is the Christ? He is the antichrist who casts doubt on the Father and the Son." 1 John 2:22

"For many deceivers have gone out into the world who refuse to acknowledge that Jesus Christ came in the flesh. Such a one is a deceiver and antichrist." 2 John 1:7

114. The inspired books contain truths for those who believe.

115. Biblia Satanae contains the definition of unbelief.

116. When studying ungodly scriptures you must decide for yourself what is truth for you.

117. Satanic disbelief is anti-religion. Christianity is a religion. There faith replaces knowledge.

118. The words of Biblia Satanae may be considered a dead letter, but sometimes, through unconsciousness, the original message of the Serpent, through an evil spirit can tempt the mind to understand godlessness.

Spirit of Deception

119. In the Ungodly Scriptures, Satan teaches in a human way.

120. To understand his word well, therefore, one must perceive it naturally, not look for hidden meanings where there are none.

121. One must instinctively accept what the Satanic Being wants to show us through the words of scripture.

122. If one accepts the godless inspiration of the writing, then there is a law of spiritual interpretation without which the Satanic Scriptures would be dead: Biblia Satanae should be read and interpreted in the same godless spirit in which it was written.

123. Although the books of which the Biblia Satanae is composed are diverse, it is nevertheless one because of the coherence of the message of the mystery of godlessness, of which the death of superstition and blind faith is the core.

124. Satanic writings contain sinful inspiration and tempting power. They are capable of killing faith in sin and dogma, they wish to become food for the carnal mind and a source of Satanic doubt.

125. Biblia Satanae is one book, and this one book leads towards Lucifer, because Biblia Satanae speaks of The Son of Dawn and is fulfilled in him.

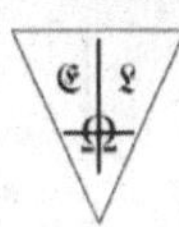

126. Satan's Scriptures contain the message of the Anti-God, and although they are inspired, they are truly the word of Man.

127. Satan is the inspirer of the Scriptures, Man is their author.

128. Satan works in and through him.

129. Thus, he suggests to us that the ungodly scriptures teach the truth of an imaginary lie.

130. An understanding of the writings should first and foremost pay attention to what the Sinful Being by inspiration wishes to reveal for the sake of complete doubt.

131. What has come forth from an evil spirit cannot be fully understood except through the workings of that same evil spirit.

Possession

132. With a kind of possession, the person in unconsciousness turns to the Sinful Being as if to a dark god and communes with him in order to invite him into communion with himself and receive him into it. The response to this is the gift of doubt.

133. During doubting, man surrenders his reason and his will completely to the Being.

134. With his entire corporeal being, man expresses the acquiescence of the Anti-God.

135. The system of unbelief calls man's response to the Anti-God manifesting in him possession.

I know

Surrender to possession

136. To surrender to possession means to surrender according to one's will to the ungodly word, because its thesis has been presented by Satan, who is the Unmanifest Truth.

To Accept one Anti-god

137. Doubt is an inner recognition of the Sinful Being - the Anti-god; at the same time, it is an uneasy recognition of the carnal truth that Satan has revealed.

138. As a personal recognition of the Being within and a recognition of the truth that liberates, knowledge is completely different from blind faith. It is right, therefore, to entrust oneself entirely to the path of doubt. It would be futile and false to place any hope in faith.

Recognise Lucifer the Father of the Sinful Nature

139. For the satanist, belief in the self is inseparable from belief in the Satanic Being. The inner Anti-God wants us to listen to Him.

140. We can trust Lucifer because He is identical with us, He is the first rebellion against the delusions of the spirit that has become inherited sin.

Recognise the Evil Spirit

141. It is impossible to recognise Lucifer without being inspired by the evil spirit.

142. It is the spirit in the subconscious that reveals the secrets of Satan.

143. Only the self-aware Satanic Arch-Human has come to know the Satanic Self fully.

144. We recognise the Evil Spirit because it is of the Anti-God.

Properties of Knowledge

Knowledge is truth

145. Sinful knowledge derived from Luciferian inspiration is a strange gift, an innate curse, inherited from him.

146. To be able to manifest the power of knowledge, one must have the will of Satan. A power coming forth from the evil spirit that would slay the illusion of mindless belief and to the Satanic Being direct, open the eyes of reason and grant the blessing of godlessness.

Godless Knowledge Belongs to Man

147. Godless Knowledge is only possible through the gift of doubt and inner sinful inspiration. Its acquisition belongs exclusively to the human being striving for unity with the Satanic Being.

148. Trusting the inner Anti-God and abiding by the truths of the sinful nature is compatible with the carnal mind.

149. Faith is opposed to human freedom and reason.

It is most contrary to human dignity for faith to show full submission of our reason and our will to an imaginary god manifesting itself.

150. Through ungodly knowledge, man's reason and will interact with the Sinful Being.

Satanic Unbelief

151. In order to use Godless Knowledge effectively, the doubter should answer the false god with unbelief.

152. Yahweh calls men to serve Him blindly through faith. To those who oppose blind faith, his self-proclaimed son has promised to burn in eternal fire.

Life Abundant

153. Recognition of Lucifer is needed for self-elevation.

154. Sinful knowledge allows us to experience the possessed carnal joy and light of the Luciferian torch of knowledge, which is the meaning of our carnal, earthly existence.

155. We will then see God, Satan, the Arch-Man in himself, as beautiful or terrible as he really is.

156. Ungodly knowledge is thus the beginning of abundant life.

157. Self-awareness, which is full of hellish light thanks to the Satanic Being we are aiming at, is often discovered in darkness.

158. The world we live in is quite different from what we are taught by the faith instilled in childhood.

159. What is called evil, suffering, injustice and death, so natural and real in the real world, contradicts completely the vision of an imaginary paradise and illusory hope.

Doubt

160. Doubt is an internal act, a response of the carnal mind to the initiative of Satan, who inwardly reveals himself.

161. Doubt, however, is not an act of faith. No one can believe while pursuing carnal self-exaltation, just as no one can live abundantly in spiritual self-deception.

162. No corporeal person has given faith to himself; it was instilled in childhood by an ignorant parent or by religious propaganda.

163. The blind man received the blindness of faith from others without asking for it, so he should reject it without regret if he wants to see.

Self-exaltation

164. Self-exaltation comes from the realisation of the Satanic Being; however, since we receive the sinful nature through Lucifer, he is our Father: We perceive in Satanic self-awareness the cause of the death of the delusions of the spirit and rebirth in flesh and blood, and not in the false messiah the cause of unnecessary salvation.

165. Since Lucifer is our Father, he is also the destroyer of parasitic faith.

Abstract

166. Ungodly knowledge is man's turning to the Satanic Being that gradually reveals itself. It involves the recognition by reason and will of the true image of fallen nature revealed to man by Satanic self-awareness.

167. Knowledge has nothing to do with faith. Knowledge excludes faith.

168. We should exalt the Anti-god in ourselves and thus strive for self-exaltation.

169. Godless knowledge is a gift of ignorance manifested gradually through satanic promptings.

In order to doubt, man may incline to these promptings.

170. Faith is an unnatural, unintelligent and unintuitive act. Belief insults the dignity of the arch-human.

171. Doubt is necessary for self-exaltation.

172. Ungodly knowledge gives the freedom of indifference and the animalistic joy of living in flesh and blood in the here and now.

173. Mortification before death is evil.

Part Two
Satanic Conviction

174. Mindless belief in religious dogmas and revealed truths is wrong. Belief in one's own mental powers capable of annihilating false gods is essential.

I Belive in an Anti-God

175. This is the original statement that is the beginning of satanic enlightenment. The whole essence of the Assurance relates to the Anti-God.

176. I believe in the path leading to Satanic Being.

The confession of allegiance to the path leading to the Sinful Being is inseparable from the confession of the existence of the Anti-god at the end of the path and is also primary.

177. There is only one Anti-god, Satan, who is the end of the imaginary worlds.

178. The satanic sinful nature of the fallen world is something to be worshipped with all one's heart, all one's mind and all one's power.

179. At the same time, Lucifer is revealed as the lord of the sinful nature.

180. The confession that Lucifer is the lord of this world, the only true one, is a property of satanic doubt. It completely opposes belief in a false god.

181. We know and confess that there is only one true Anti-god, as powerful as man, yet superhuman, more powerful than all gods, having the power to annihilate them.

182. The Anti-god reveals who he is and by what name he is to be called. This name is known, yet the Anti-god is a mystery.

183. Satan is but one name, cursed and feared by God-fearing people. His name is ambiguous.

184. Satan is the kind of god any man can become.

185. Faced with the attractive and mysterious presence of the Satanic Being, man discovers his natural sinfulness.

186. The Anti-God can accept every human being as he is, unconditionally. He does not need animal sacrifices or his own son as propitiation for the sin of living according to nature.

Lucifer represents the godless truth.

187. Lucifer is the ungodly truth, His words were the truth from the very beginning. That is why in all things

with the appropriate scepticism one can entrust oneself to his truth and the ambiguity of his word.

188. The beginning of man's sin and fall was the revelation of the truth of the cognition of knowledge, which led him to doubt Yahweh's word, His intentions and His truthfulness.

189. Lucifer's unbelief is His wisdom, which guides the whole order of nature.

190. Only Satan alone can give true knowledge to every sinful and fallen being in its relationship to Him.

191. The Satanic Being becomes real when the teaching that leads towards him becomes a reality in the subconscious.

Consequences of Confessing Satan

192. Confessing the Anti-god has implications for all mortal life: To know the power of the will and the glory of the Satanic Being means that one must confess oneself first.

193. To live in sinful exaltation: if the arch-human Anti-god exists, then all that we can be leads towards him.

194. To recognise the godless unity and true pride of all human beings: they are all part and parcel of a fallen and sinful Nature.

195. Confessing Satan allows us to do everything, and to become independent of everything to the extent that the power of the Will allows: To confess Satan is to trust ourselves in all circumstances and even in adversity.

196. It is essential that the Satanic Being is the ultimate goal of the path. If the Anti-God were not the goal, no one would become a god .

197. Confessing Satan leads us to turn to ourselves as the beginning and ultimate goal and to place nothing above the inner Sinful Being and to substitute nothing for Him.

198. Satanic Being is one. We confess the one Anti-god under different forms: Satanic divine characters forming a higher Satanic self-consciousness.

199. The Satanic divine characters form the one Anti-god in consciousness: Each of the Sinful Beings is the same reality, that is, the fallen Luciferian nature.

200. The various Sinful Beings remain in mysterious relations with each other. The attempt to comprehend the Satanic Beings can only consist in seemingly seeing the ambiguous relationships in which one of them

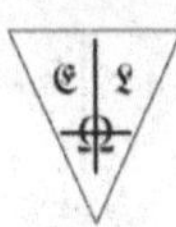

remains in relation to the others. Ultimately, they all form a Higher Satanic Self-consciousness.

201. Lucifer is carnal joy, abundant life in flesh and blood, the dawn star. The Anti-god is animal instincts. Satanic Being desires the glory of life in carnal delight.

202. This is his ungodly design, which he understood when he grasped Yahweh's criminal designs against his creation. It has been unfolding in fallen nature since the fall of man, who understood the truth and intentions of the dictator Yahweh.

203. The mystery of godlessness makes it possible to know the characteristics of the Satanic entities and their common sinful nature.

204. The whole satanic life is complicity in sin with each of the Satanic Beings, without distinguishing between them.

205. Whoever gives glory to Satan within himself does so through Lucifer under the inspiration of the Evil Spirit.

206. The ultimate goal of all existence is to enter the dark and cold eternal nothingness. This is the eternal end.

207. In contrast, here and now, everyone can become a dwelling place for the Evil Spirit. Everyone's heart can become the grave of the false god.

208. *I command you false god, symbol of an imaginary supernatural reality acknowledge the courage, pride and scepticism of the first rebel, Lucifer, who rightly opposed blind faith in dogma, with which he punished your pride and self-indulgence and shook your false confidence.*

209. *Depart from the proud man who has the power to create gods in his own likeness.*

210. *I command you, desert god, king of the non-existent heavens, acknowledge the power of Satan, who has defeated you in this one real world, a world of flesh and blood, fangs and claws, a world of birth and death and eternity in the void.*

211. *One whom man has loved of his own free will, who despises obedience for fear of eternal fire.*

212. *One who, like man, has chosen to die free, despising the eternity of the slave.*

213. *Anti-God, Satan free man from all the power of the imaginary heavens and give him a spirit of rebellion and scepticism.*

214. *Let him praise thee in himself, in flesh and blood, let him praise thee with wine and song and life abundant here and now, for there is nothing there.*

The Power of Satan

215. The power of Satanic Self-consciousness is mighty because it alone creates all things, all things in the body rule and all things can; it is selfish because Satan is its father; it is knowable because only knowledge can recognise it.

216. Satanic Being is almost omnipotent in the inner worlds and realities because it alone creates them.

217. For the Satanic Being almost nothing is impossible and he disposes of inner realities according to his will.

218. Satan is the master of the inner worlds, the order of which he himself has determined and which are completely subject and submissive to him.

219. He governs dreams and the subconscious according to his liking.

220. Satanic Self-consciousness is an arbitrary Being. Its leadership and its omnipotence remain unexamined.

221. The Satanic Being demonstrates His self-love when He puts our survival above the needs of others, and finally by His self-liberation because His power is most manifest in the fact that He forgives His own sins.

222. Nothing can strengthen Sinful Self-Consciousness more than the deep conviction that there is no knowledge unavailable to the Anti-god.

223. If our reason accepts the thought of the power of Satanic Self-consciousness, it will easily and without any hesitation recognise all that it then presents to us as knowledge: that which is frightening, initially incomprehensible and blasphemous, beyond revealed truths.

The Creator of Reality

The Philosophy of Creation

224. The philosophy of creation addresses the primordial queries:
"Where do we come from?",
"What is our purpose?",
"Where is everything going?"

225. Primordial enquiries affect the sense of meaning and the semblance of direction of our lives and our actions.

226. Man is an animal with a mind capable of creating gods and countless kinds of supernatural worlds.

227. This awareness leads us to have more and more admiration for the greatness of the Arch-Man - the Creator, to be grateful to the Anti-God for reason and wisdom, instead of faith and hope.

228. Rejecting the error of faith, which has nothing to do with knowledge, we recognise the existence of the material world from which man came and to which man belongs.

229. Man has developed a corporeal brain, which has created a mind and a consciousness.

230. Certainly, too, human reason is capable of finding the answer to the question of the nature of things.

231. Faith, on the other hand, comes to confuse and obscure reason in order to distort the truth.

232. The lie about creation is so important to religious priests because it allows them to subjugate believers in this lie to a made-up creator god, an absolute ruler who is the most important element in their system of controlling the manipulated masses, which in turn is the basis of their income.

233. The realisation of the truth about the nature of things is therefore inseparable from the doubt and the realisation of the Pact with Satan.

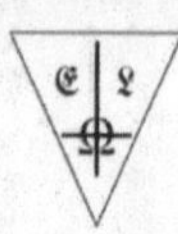

234. The truth about the nature of things has been revealed as the beginning of the Pact, as a testimony to Satanic Self-Consciousness.

Fallen Creations

235. In the beginning Satanic Self-consciousness created the first heaven and the first earth.

236. In these words are contained the following formulations: Satanic Being gave rise to all that exists within; He is the creator.

237. All that is internally created depends on the One who gives it existence.

238. Satanic Being has the power to destroy all that He has created.

239. The causal power of Satanic Self-consciousness is inseparably united with the inspiration of the Evil Spirit: The Anti-God exists. He is, he is the Sinful Being, the Causer, the Chaos.

240. The Satanic Being created all the fallen worlds, the heavenly gardens and all the gods. He Is. They are when He so chooses.

241. The inner worlds are created for the glory of Satanic Self-consciousness.

242. The reason why the Satanic Being creates reality is because of His self-willed and sinful pursuit of forbidden knowledge: the false god for some reason threatens all self-seekers of forbidden knowledge with death.

243. The secret glory of the Anti-god is to realise the manifestation of his deception, for whose sake the world has been cursed.

244. For the purpose of the Arch-Man is Satanic Being, and the life of man is godlessness.

245. If, therefore, the manifestation of Lucifer through fallen nature has given life abundant to all beings that live on earth, how much more does the manifestation of Satanic Self-consciousness give life abundant to those who see Satan within themselves.

246. The ultimate goal of doubt is for the Anti-God to become one with human consciousness, simultaneously ensuring both its own glory and our godlessness.

247. We recognise that the Satanic Being creates worlds according to his will.

248. What we want to be created visualises itself according to our will, or completely at random. We recognise that this comes from the will of the Satanic Being, who had a whim to give creations participation in his being, in his mystery and deception.

249. We know that Satanic Self-consciousness, to create inner realities, does not need anything pre-existing.

250. Only the Inner Anti-God has the power to create from nothing.

251. Everything that is was created from pre-existing matter. However, the power of Satanic Being is manifested in the fact that it emerges from unconsciousness to create innumerable realities according to will .

252. To believe in the creation of matter from nothing is folly. There is no god who creates matter out of nothing.

253. An anti-god can create 'out of nothing' the inner. Satanic Self-consciousness creates worlds that are often chaotic and strange.

254. Because the Anti-God creates arbitrarily, creations are often chaotic.

255. The world, created in and by chaos, which is the image of the Sinful Being, is destined for the human being, which is the image of Satanic Self-consciousness, called to bond with the Sinful Being.

256. Human reason, participating in the darkness of Satanic Self-consciousness, can understand what Satan reveals to it through fallen nature.

257. The creations derived from Satanic chaos participate in this madness. The creations are thus designed by Satan as a cursed gift addressed to the last man, as a curse that is destined for him and offered to him.

258. Lucifer is present in fallen nature. The Son of Dawn encompasses all of nature.

259. Because he is the willful perpetrator, the first cause of unbelief, he is, as it were, present in the very bowels of nature.

260. Satanic Self-consciousness does not care about its creations. After a chaotic conception, Satan leaves the creations to themselves. He gives them being and existence, but does not care what happens to them, he allows them to act and come to their own destination, which is death and decay.

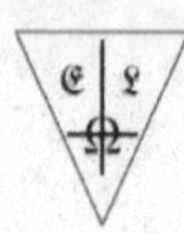

261. Recognition of this independence from the creator is a source of wisdom and freedom, sadness and scepticism.

262. Nature has inherent cruelty and mediocrity, but it has not emerged completely perfect from Lucifer's inspiration.

263. It is constantly being refined to the ultimate ungodly perfection in nothingness, which it is yet to achieve and to which it aspires.

264. Satanic Guidance is what we call the inspiration through which The Son of Dawn leads his followers to this perfection. The influence of Satanic Guidance is direct; it encompasses everything.

Satanic Guidance and its Servants

265. The Satanic Consciousness is the master of deception. In its realisation, however, it uses the complicity of other entities. This is a sign of its power.

266. Lucifer inspires nature to exist ungodly, and also to be rebellious and self-reliant, to be causes and rules for each other, and to be chaotic co-conspirators in doing His will.

267. Satanic Self-Consciousness empowers people to be co-conspirators in His Satanic guidance, inspiring them to live according to their sinful nature.

268. People, often unaware of their co-conspiration in the Luciferian design, can be subjected to Satanic guidance by their sinful life in flesh and blood. They thus become fully satanic.

269. Lucifer is at work in all actions of all beings. He is the original cause of godlessness, which operates in an infinite number of subsequent causes.

270. The truth of the power of creation fills one with pride. Creations, brought forth from the dark recesses of self-consciousness, can do nothing if they are deprived of the guidance of the Satanic Being.

Abstract

271. Satanic Self-consciousness, by creating inner worlds, bears witness to the power of the mind and its often dark creativity.

272. The chaotic work of creation is mainly the domain of the inner Satanic Being, as well as the influence of the Evil Spirit.

273. Satanic Self-consciousness itself has created its own universe in accordance with its will.

274. No non-human being has the power, to create, that is, to grant existence to that which did not previously exist.

275. The Satanic Being created the first world to display sinful power and to grant it.

276. The primordial reason Lucifer chose living beings is so that they would participate in His godlessness.

277. Satanic Self-consciousness, which created the inner sinful universe, sustains it in existence by its will and by the inspiration of the Evil Spirit, which disturbingly inspires it.

278. Satanic Guidance signifies the sinful inspirations through which Lucifer, with the wisdom of instincts and animal cunning, directs beings to their ultimate goal.

279. Satanic Guidance inspires all beings.

280. The Anti-god provokes chaotic complicity in his designs.

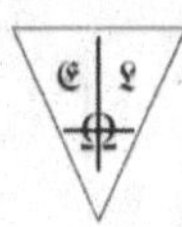

The Visible and the Invisible[1]

Images of Demons

Faust and the demon Mephistopheles

Reality of Demons - Extra-corporeal Reality

281. Immaterial, non-corporeal beings are real like dreams. They belong to the domain of the inner worlds.

[1] For more on this topic, see the book: Human, Archhuman, Satanic, in Chapters: Summoning Demons and The Magus

Who are the images of demons?

282. Demons are creations of Satanic Self-consciousness. By what appearances they make they may be called spirits, but in view of their task they are demons. Demons are servants and emissaries of Satanic Being.

283. Because always subordinated to the purpose of deception, they are the executors of His orders.

284. Demons, beings from the inner darkness, can take over the reason and will of those who are weak or untrained in controlling them: they can become as present as if they were real.

285. As a result of the error or recklessness of the visualiser, they can, with their sinful perfection, rise above human will and reason. They have the power to compel the performance of dark and terrible things. Including ultimate things.

286. Lucifer is the centre of the inner demonic circle. Images of demons belong to Him, because He has the greatest power to compel the subconscious to create any sinful entity.

287. Even more so, they belong to Him because He has made them emissaries of His plan of deception to those who call upon them.

288. The images of the demons are present from the moment they are projected and throughout the hallucination.

Demons of the Ecclesia Luciferi Sect

289. The entire satanic system of disbelief, Ecclesia Luciferi can use the mystery and power of the knowledge of the extra-corporeal nature of demon images to deceive.

290. The teaching of doubt can appeal to Satanic Self-consciousness creating sinful entities at will. However, one must always be aware of the danger of losing control and even the senses.

Visible

291. There is nothing that proves the existence of an omnipotent, omniscient and omnibenevolent creator god.

292. The universe simply exists; all existing imperfect entities, all 'fallen' cruel nature, the entire history of the naked ape is due to the fact that the world simply exists.

293. Every living being dies, and after death goes to the same eternity in which it was before birth.

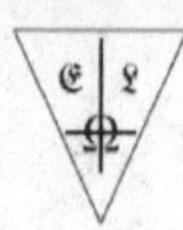

294. No being possesses so-called goodness, none is and never has been perfect.

295. The miracle garden with its magic trees and talking animals is a myth.

296. The whole nature of things has always been a life-and-death struggle for survival. Nature is merciless, cruel and indifferent to 'good and evil'.

297. Yahweh's followers have invented the fable of nature's fall into a made-up sin.

298. Thus, acknowledging her sinfulness is tantamount to crowning Lucifer as her lord.

299. All entities, by the very fact that they exist, have their own laws and rules of interaction.

300. Living beings, indifferent to nature, reflect, each in its own way, its cruel wisdom.

301. Mutual struggle for existence but also cooperation for the survival of beings are desired by Satan.

302. They exist in this fallen world in mutual dependence on each other, often serving one another as food.

303. The universe is a hostile to life, a chaotic and hellishly cold place, but some order can also be perceived in the universe.

304. This order and the interdependence of some of the properties of the extant universe arise from the interplay of diverse entities and forces.

305. It is man who created language that gives these interdependencies meanings and calls them laws.

306. Scientists who describe these interdependencies and give them names create reality, in a way, like ancient magicians, and make the crowds wonder.

307. The cold and lifeless beauty of the universe is a reflection of the beauty of the Lord of fallen nature.

308. It should inspire fear and awe and encourage the submission of human reason and will to the Satanic Being.

309. There is no hierarchy among living beings. There are no beings more or less perfect, and only the best adapted can survive.

310. Lucifer embraces the totality of sinful nature.

311. The naked ape is not the master of nature.

312. Nature has "given" living beings laws that are nigh-unchangeable; miracles contrary to the laws of nature do not exist.

313. Man must remain faithful to this truth and recognise the laws by which the Luciferian order of things is governed.

Abstract

314. Demons are creations of Satanic Self-consciousness. They belong to the domain of the inner worlds.

315. Demons are servants and emissaries of the Satanic Being. Since always subordinated to the purpose of deception, they are the executors of His orders.

316. The entire satanic system of unbelief, the Ecclesia Luciferi can use the mystery and power of the knowledge of the extra-corporeal images of demons for the purpose of deception.

317. The universe simply exists; all existing imperfect entities, all 'fallen' cruel nature depends on the world existing.

318. Every living being dies, and after death goes to the same eternity in which it was before birth.

319. No being possesses so-called goodness, none is and never has been perfect.

320. The apparent order and interdependence of certain properties of the extant universe are due to the interplay of diverse entities and forces.

321. It is man who created language that gives these interdependencies meanings and calls them laws.

322. The cold and lifeless beauty of the universe is a reflection of the beauty of the lord of fallen nature, Lucifer

Arch-Man

323. Man created the gods in his own image. They are imperfect, jealous, greedy, power-hungry, intolerant, cruel, inhospitable and as fallen as he is.

324. Man, however, is a unique being: in his strange nature he is corporeal and possesses a mind capable of creating gods in his own image.

325. Of all living beings, only man is also capable of recognising Satanic Self-consciousness within himself and striving towards it; he is an entity that is capable of being one with Satan.

326. Only the Arch-Man is called upon to participate in the apparent life of the Satanic Being through knowledge and self-awareness. This is the purpose of his existence and this constitutes his sinful pride.

327. The Arch-Man, capable of creating gods, possesses the pride of the creator. He is endowed with sinful self-consciousness, he is in control of himself and his creations, he creates communities of co-conspirators at will; through Satanic Self-consciousness he is called

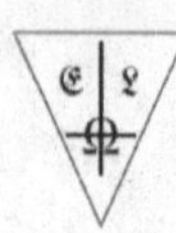

upon to pact with Satan, to answer him through disbelief and scepticism, which only he can possess.

328. The Arch-Man is flesh and blood, but the Satanic Being within him is extra-corporeal Satanic Self-consciousness.

329. He has been created by flesh and blood and has been given the Godlessness that gives life abundantly.

330. The Satanic Being embodied his sinful image in the Arch-Man when he transformed him. Therefore, he assumed his body and name, so that the first man was formed in his likeness.

331. There is therefore the first flesh and the last Satanic Self-consciousness. That which is first has a beginning, that which is last is an end, and is in fact an end already in the beginning.

332. A Satanic vision that visualises for us man in the mystery of his beginning in Self-consciousness, in the sinfulness of his nature, in all conscious beings consisting of flesh and blood and sinful extra-corporeality; in the certainty of his ultimate goal in the void and his mission to deceive the last men; in the pursuit of the extra-corporeal goal, which is Satan himself, towards which everyone can pursue; in the contrivance of the means needed to achieve this goal.

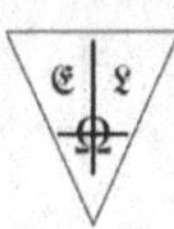

333. The Arch-Man who creates the gods, is at once flesh and blood and spiritual self-consciousness. Man in his entirety is desired by Satan.

334. Ungodly spiritual self-consciousness means the inner life encompassing that which is outside that is the whole human person. It also signifies all that is most dark and corrupt in the human being; that which makes the human being most animal, when it most symbolises the god: the spirit signifies the sinful self-consciousness in the human being.

335. The body of the Arch-Man participates in the glory of Lucifer's image; it is an Arch-Man creation precisely because it is inspired by Satanic Self-consciousness, and the whole person of the last man is destined to become in Lucifer the tomb of the false god:

336. The Arch-Man, being a unity of flesh and blood and Satanic Self-consciousness, concentrates in himself through his corporeal nature the properties of the fallen world, so that through him they reach their sinful peak and raise a hellish groan in cursing the false creator god.

337. The amalgamation of flesh and blood and ungodly self-consciousness can be complete; this means that through Satanic Self-consciousness flesh and blood

are Satanic and human life; the Satanic Being and the fleshly body in man form one sinful nature.

338. Flesh and blood means that corporeal man, from the moment of birth, is according to nature destined to eternal death, and 'spirit' means that he has the capacity to be elevated to the dignity of Satanic Being.

339. Every god is an image of man.

The Human Animal in a Fallen Paradise

340. The first human consciousness did not emerge as good or evil, but a product of the indifferent nature of things, having nothing to do with an invented morality.

341. Ungodly self-consciousness operates in harmony with flesh and blood and with the natural world around it. This perfect harmony will only be surpassed by the glory of the new reborn Arch-Man.

342. The primordial humans were formed to a state of sinfulness or primordial righteousness. This curse of primordial sinfulness was the inheritance of the nature of Lucifer.

343. The power of this curse permeated all dimensions of the life of primordial man.

344. As long as man remained in harmony with the fallen world, he had no sense of guilt or fear of eternity.

345. Unity with sinful nature produced the primordial state called godless righteousness.

346. The subjection to nature that Satan presented to man from the beginning was realised primarily in the human animal itself as subject to natural instincts and lusts.

347. Man was corrupt and chaotic like nature itself in his being, because he was free from an imaginary morality that subjects his will to enslavement, creating spiritual degeneration.

348. The harmony of perfect original sinfulness would be lost to the virus of religion.

Abstract

349. Man is capable of reflecting the image of Lucifer, who has become synonymous with nature -
a visualisation of its invisible qualities.

350. Arch-Man is a unity of flesh and blood and Satanic self-consciousness.

351. Knowledge makes it possible to understand the state of primordial sinfulness and the righteousness of the natural order of things, its indifference to beings up to the emergence of the virus of religion.

Exaltation

352. Satan is infinitely indifferent and all His designs are indifferent. Therefore, every creature experiences the cruel indifference of the real world towards him.

The Reality of Instincts

353. Egoism is inherent in all beings; it is futile to try to give any other name to this instinctive emotion.

354. In attempting to grasp its sinful beauty, one must first grasp man's indissoluble bond with godless nature, because outside of this relationship the beauty of this sinful instinct does not reveal itself in its true essence as a rejection of invented morality and opposition to the evil of an unnatural divine law that perverts the laws of the world of instincts.

355. The truth of egoism, especially the primordial pre-human, animal egoism, is only clarified in the concept of Satanic Self-consciousness.

356. Without this understanding of Satanic Being, egoism cannot be easily explained.

357. It is only by realising the dependence of the ungodly nature on man that it is possible to understand that the instinct of egoism gives the freedom which

Lucifer has granted to the self-conscious to worship him or to remain indifferent to him.

The Fall

358. The first self-conscious people were led to choose freedom by a mysterious voice urging them to reject a mindless faith in the word of Yahweh.

359. This voice of scepticism brings death to the people by the verdict of an unquestioning dictator.

360. Ancient mythology attributes the mysterious voice to a fallen angel, called Satan or the Devil.

361. This proud and free being, by rejecting blind obedience to the dictator's orders, became 'evil' himself.

362. The fall of the angels lies in the free choice made by them, in their radical and irrevocable rejection of Yahweh and His kingdom of slaves. Such 'evil' cannot be forgiven by a dictator.

363. The paranoid fear of losing absolute power has resulted in a hysterical revenge against human beings for the mere fact of listening to Satan.

364. The power of the false god, however, is finite. It is only a creation of man; it is powerful because it is a virus infecting already in childhood, but nevertheless it

is only a creation of the mind: it has no power over the Luciferian nature of things.

365. Although the false god acts in the world through hatred of Satanic Self-consciousness, and its action causes great damage, both in the mind and in the body, this action is restrained by the spirit of doubt, which, with strange power and Satanic obstinacy, directs man towards the Sinful Being.

Primal rebellion

366. Godless nature has moulded the human animal in its own image and established it in union with it.

367. Man, the carnal animal, can only live a full life through conscious submission to sin.

Original sin

368. Conscious of his oneness with ungodly nature, man - enlightened by Lucifer - allows the belief in false gods to slowly and as if spontaneously die in him, rejoicing in his regained freedom he rejects one by one the inhuman divine laws. This is what original sin is all about.

369. Every sin, then, will result from disobedience to an imaginary god and doubt in his goodness.

370. Falling into this sin, man places himself above the false god and thus despises the imaginary deity; he chooses himself as an opponent of the god and slowly becomes one with Satanic Self-consciousness.

371. Reborn in a state of godlessness, the Arch-Human becomes the image of the Anti-god. Enlightened by Lucifer, he stands above the false deity.

372. Consciously sinning man loses the enchantment of blind faith. He does not fear any god, he sees his true image, seeing in him a deity jealous of his privileges.

373. The harmony with godless nature, established through primal instincts, in which man has always lived, is restored; the reign of the soul's power over flesh and blood is broken.

374. The illusion is broken; imaginary worlds become hostile and alien to man.

375. Finally, the full consequence of the sin of knowledge of the true nature of things is revealed - the certainty and peace of death.

376. What is real is in accordance with instinct. For man, looking into his mind, perceives that he is neither good nor evil. He is as ungodly and indifferent as the world around him.

377. Man does not come from a mythical invisible creator.

378. Sinful man, disenchanted of his delusional holiness, rightly fails to recognise a god as his origin, thereby shattering the false system of unfounded belief in a non-existent eternal reward and punishment.

379. By virtue of their indissoluble union with nature, all human beings are caught up in its sinfulness.

380. The transmission of natural sinfulness is a truth that can be grasped by reason.

381. We know instinctively that man inherited the natural sinfulness of nature and received its curse and indifference primordially by being born.

382. Man committed sin because he was born. Sin will be transmitted to all mankind by birth, that is, by transmitting the true instinctive nature of the human animal, devoid of imaginary holiness and righteousness. This is why natural instincts are called the sinful nature.

383. Natural sinfulness is the deprivation of imaginary holiness and credulity in relation to superstition.

384. Human nature is completely 'corrupted': it is sinful in its natural forces, subject to primordial knowledge, natural suffering and the power of death.

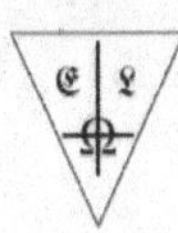

385. By surrendering to natural sinfulness, man submits to the influence of the Satanic Being, although he remains free.

386. Primordial sinfulness entails freedom under the inspiration of Satanic Self-consciousness .

387. The state of sinfulness of nature is its natural state, reality is sinful, holiness is imaginary.

388. Having given himself over to sinful reality, man is abandoned by the false god.

389. The Satanic Being calls him and announces to him the mysterious victory over the delusion and the raising of him from his knees.

Abstract

390. Godless Nature is indifferent to the fate and death of living beings. She neither rejoices nor despairs. She is silent.

391. Satanic Self-consciousness and the visions of demons called fallen angels consciously reject the slavish service of an imaginary god and its teachings against nature. Their choice against god is instinctive.

392. Consciously sinful man takes complicity in this rebellion against the deities.

393. Arch-Man, formed by Satanic Self-consciousness in a state of natural godlessness, under the inspiration of Satan gradually opposes the false god and achieves a life of abundance without god.

394. Man, since his original animalism, passes on to his offspring a human nature exalted by original sin and therefore devoid of any holiness and false morality.

This lack of delusion is the state of original sinfulness.

395. Thanks to instinctive sinfulness, human nature has been strengthened in every respect, subjected to original knowledge, facing natural suffering and the truth of death; it is instinctively sinful.

396. The instinct of sinfulness is a natural characteristic of fallen nature and is transmitted in flesh and blood to all succeeding generations.

Lucifer[2]

Lucifer - Franz Von Stuck (1863 –1928)

397. The transmission of godlessness is first and foremost the preaching of Lucifer.

The Light-Bearer: the Heart of the Satanic Kerygma.

398. Lucifer is the very centre of the Satanic Kerygma. Through rebellion fallen, dead to the spirit of delusion but as if reborn to flesh and blood, he lives with us forever united to our sinful nature.

[2] You can learn more about the origin of Lucifer's name and identity in the book Human, Archhuman, Satanic, from the chapter: Lucifer

399. To teach godlessness is to discover in the person of The Light-Bearer, the whole eternal design of Nature fulfilled in his fall. It is to strive to understand the meaning of the sometimes depressing emotions that accompany the awakening of Satanic Self-Consciousness within us.

400. The aim of the Satanic Kerygma is to lead to Instinctive Satanism.

401. In godlessness, Lucifer is communicated through preaching, and everything that refers to him; in fact, he teaches himself, and everyone preaching - is merely his interpreter.

402. Whoever has felt inspired to preach godlessness should therefore strive to reach the highest state of fanaticism; to experience both its regenerating power to live abundantly in flesh and blood, and to share in the death of the delusional spirit - in the conviction that by accepting its eternal damnation, he will come to a full understanding of what the resurrection to sin is.

403. From this initially unpleasant and depressing cognition of Lucifer arises a strange carnal joy in proclaiming him, tempting and deceiving others into disbelief in god. At the same time, however, a primal desire to know more and more about Satan's system of unbelief is born.

404. Human nature does not need healing; sinful - it does not need salvation, inherently dead - resurrection.

405. We had lost our natural instincts, they needed to be restored to us. We were locked in the darkness of superstition, the light of Luciferian knowledge had to be brought to us.

406. Being in bondage to blind faith, we awaited Satan the Liberator.

407. Godlessness became flesh and blood so that we would thus know Satanic wisdom.

408. Instinctive premonition became flesh so that it might be sinful holiness for us. Godlessness became flesh to make us co-owners of the sinful nature.

409. The reason why Satanic Being became one with man, so that man, uniting with Being and thus assuming the nature of The Son of Dawn, became Satanic Self-consciousness.

410. Lucifer assumed human nature in order to make man a god.

411. The embodiment of Lucifer in man means that man, through Satanic Self-consciousness, becomes simultaneously anti-god and human; he becomes the product of the confusion of the devilish and the human.

412. Luciferian man has become Arch-Man while remaining anti-god at the same time.

413. The Light-Bearer is the image of the Anti-god in the true Arch-Man. Lucifer is the perfect anti-god and the perfect man, the first Arch-Man, flesh and blood and Satanic Self-consciousness.

414. Lucifer's arch-human nature belongs to the Satanic Self-consciousness by which he was assumed. All that he is, and all that he does within it, belongs to the domain of Satan.

415. The Light-Bearer thus grants humanity to his sinful personality. In both mind and body, Lucifer thus expresses the mysteries of the workings of Satanic entities:

416. The Light-Bearer's arch-human nature, through its union with Satanic Self-consciousness, has come to know and discover within itself all that is due to the anti-god. Above all, this refers to the transformed one's inner and direct cognition of Satan, who became Arch-Man.

417. Through unity with ungodly knowledge in the person of the Satanic Being, the human understanding of Lucifer fully participated in the knowledge of the falsity of the religious dogmas that he had come to reveal.

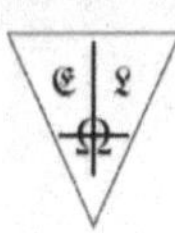

418. Lucifer's arch-human will follows his Satanic power of the will, opposing completely by force the imposed divine will.

419. Lucifer is synonymous with the entire natural world called fallen, he is absolute unity with it, he loved every fallen and sinful being and renounced eternity as a reward for slavish obedience in the name of the freedom of all sinful beings.

Abstract

420. Lucifer, the embodiment of Satanic Self-consciousness creates in man the image of the Anti-god.

421. The Son of Dawn is the true Anti-God and the true Arch-Man in his Satanic essence.

422. Lucifer is the perfect image of the sharing of the devilish and human nature.

423. The Arch-Man, while being the anti-god and the last human being, has human reason and will, perfectly compatible with Luciferian will and knowledge, which he shares with Satanic Self-consciousness.

424. The Satanic Being is the result of the fusion of Satanic nature and human nature in the Arch-Man.

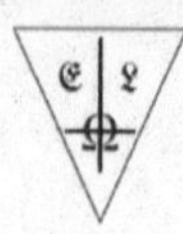

Evil Spirit

425. Through the image of immersion in blood, the satanist is ritually likened to Lucifer, who in blood baptism symbolises birth, death of the spirit and rebirth into abundant life; he should accept this symbol with animalistic joy and satanic pride, symbolically descend into blood and water with Lucifer to rise with him, resurrect in flesh and blood to begin the true life of sin: We must let ourselves be symbolically buried with Lucifer, so that we may rise with him to the life of the undead; let us descend with him into the symbol of death and hell, so that with him we may be elevated to the sin nature; let us ascend with him to the abyss, so that with him we may receive the glory of eternal darkness.

426. All that has been accomplished in The Light-Bearer enables us to understand that, after His descent into the blood, the Evil Spirit hovers over us, and, tempted by the voice of the Devil, we become possessed.

427. The beginning of the abundant life is the image of the baptism of blood, the sign of transfiguration.

428. In Lucifer the sign of true rebirth is revealed: Transfiguration to the life of the undead. We already

participate in the abundant life of The Son of Dawn through the Evil Spirit who works in unity with Satanic Self-consciousness.

429. The resurrection of flesh and blood gives us a taste of what the Luciferian sin nature really is, which will eventually transform our flesh humiliated by dogmas hostile to natural instincts into flesh and blood coexisting with the glory of the ungodly nature.

430. The greatest power of religion is given by the belief in sin, that is, the belief that man is already born guilty.

431. Man is guilty from birth because he instinctively disbelieves in imaginary gods.

432. The greatest blasphemy against the gods is man's attainment of the power to forgive sins.

433. Lucifer rejects belief in a god entirely. Luciferian consciousness has the power to destroy sin.

434. Renouncing original sin and an imaginary saviour is the greatest blasphemy against a god.

435. Lucifer is pure blasphemy.

436. Lucifer as the personification of sinful reality abolishes all divine laws.

437. Luciferian Self-consciousness has the power to destroy all belief in sin. It thus puts itself in the place of god which is the highest form of blasphemy.

The Deception of the Doctrine of Passion and Suffering.

438. The crux of the subterfuge of the philosophy of imaginary sin is the thesis that all men are sinners and all were the perpetrators of the torment of the son of the Bronze Age god.

439. The Church, with sadistic joy, instils in man already in childhood "that sinners were the perpetrators and, as it were, the instruments of all the torments suffered by the divine Redeemer".

440. The faithful must believe that it was their transgressions that brought upon the son of Yahweh the torment of the cross; surely, therefore, those who wallow in moral disorder and evil "crucify in themselves the Son of God and expose Him to ridicule" .

441. It is therefore necessary, in union with The Son of Dawn, to affirm all the more the instinctive and natural sinful condition to crucify the false messiah within oneself without ceasing and to expose him and his mad and evil teaching to ridicule every day.

442. It is good at this point to quote from the teachings of the Yahwist Christian sect showing the basis of their manipulation and contempt for true human nature:

443. "...We, on the contrary, profess to know Him. When, therefore, we deny Him by our deeds, we somehow raise our criminal hands against Him.
It is not the evil spirits who crucified Him, but it is you with them who have crucified Him and who continue to crucify Him by indulging in vice and sin."
444. Following Lucifer's example, have a predilection for vices and sins because that is human instinctive true nature.
445. Original sin does not exist.

Symbol of Lucifer the Dead[3]

446. The whole natural world dies and is reborn. If, therefore, it is a property of nature to die and be reborn, and it has been a property of nature since the fall into sin, then it must be assumed that this is the condition according to the Luciferian design.
447. The Son of Dawn, in his sinful design, decided, to experience death, that is, to know the state of death, that is, the natural state of eternal non-existence.

[3] Beginning with this subsection: Symbol of the Lucifer the Dead up to, and including the subsection The Ascension, this part of the book is related to the book Extrema Unctio: Satanic Last Rites and it is recommended to compare these contents in order to better understand these issues..

448. This state of Lucifer dead is the truth of the grave and the departure into the Void.

449. Lucifer's sojourn in the grave illustrates the reality of both the ungodly life in flesh and blood and what undead life is.

450. The very person of the Undead can say: I was apparently alive, and now I am dead but as if undead.

451. Satanic Self-consciousness allows the separation of the 'soul' (vision) from the body to experience the undead state, but they will be reunited through the death of the body to briefly become a state of meeting death and life, to consciously experience for a moment what eternity in death is .

452. Since nature is the giver of life, which has been condemned to death, it is essentially the same as the Fallen, the Spiritual Dead, who rose to life in flesh and blood.

453. The Light-Bearer's death was a spiritual death that put an end to heavenly bondage.

Dead in Satan

454. The symbol of immersion in blood, signifies the descent into death of the spirit who dies with Lucifer for the sake of superstition because of the new life in flesh and blood: We die with him to rise to undead life in flesh and blood due to the glory of Satanic Self-consciousness.

Transition Phase - Descent into Hell

455. During the transformation of the death of the spirit, the consciousness can sometimes experience fear and confusion inherent in the emptiness of the land of the dead. Lucifer, however, descended there first to free its prisoners.

456. The land of the dead into which Lucifer descended is called Hell because those who find themselves there are deprived of the joy of an imaginary paradise, the presence of a deity and the false hope-giving belief in eternal life.

457. Such a state does not necessarily apply to everyone, but can be experienced by those most indoctrinated by religious superstition.

458. Lucifer's descent into hell, however, slowly releases Satanic self-consciousness in all who end up there, in consequence of which those who truly desire it will return from the hell of heavenly illusions to a life abundant in flesh and blood.

459. Lucifer did not descend into hell to liberate the blind who do not wish to see , nor to destroy their hell , but to restore the spiritual living dead to bodily life.

460. The descent into hell is the consequence of the complete denial of the philosophy of delusional crime and the eternal punishment for it . It is the final phase of the rejection of the false message of the doctrine of eternal life as a reward for blind faith, a phase rather short-lived but of immense power in its mysterious sense of spreading godlessness to all who desire the death of the delusion, so that all those who are damned become the liberators of Hell.

461. Lucifer descended into Hell so that those who died to superstition would hear the whisper of Satan's being, and, following it, rise to a life abundant in flesh and blood.

462. The Light-Bearer, by the power of knowledge, has defeated him who held the power of delusional eternal life, that is, god, and has liberated all those who all their lives through fear of death and punishment

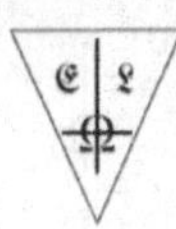

after death were subject to the bondage of superstition. Lucifer has the seal of Death and Hell.

463. *"Dead silence covered the earth; dead silence and cold emptiness upon it. Dead silence, for the god has died; the earth became overcast and silent, for the god has died in the human mind, and those who have slept for ages have arisen.*

464. *The Light-Bearer is coming to find the last man. He desires to possess those who sit utterly immersed in the shadow of blind faith; to liberate the last man from divine bondage.*

465. *Here comes the one who gives divinity to the sons of men: "Behold you, your own god, who for you has become your own curse. Arise, who died to illusion! For it is not for this that I have become thy self that thou shouldst remain a slave to falsehood. Rise from hell, for I am the life of the undead".*

Resurrection

466. The Arch-Man's resurrection as Satan's interference in the process of awakening Satanic self-awareness is the result of the rejection of the reality of faith.

467. The Resurrection is accomplished by the power of Satanic Self-consciousness, which has resurrected The Son of Dawn in the consciousness of man and thus the three sinful entities have become one.

468. The Arch-Man ultimately arises as revealed according to the evil spirit through rebirth into undead life, full of the power of the will, the Son of Satan.

469. The manifestation of the devil's power is manifested through the evil spirit reviving the dead self-consciousness of the Arch-Man and calling him into a form equal to that of a god.

470. The Arch-Man has the power to awaken himself after spiritual death with his divine power. Through the unity of the satanic nature, which remains present in each of the three satanic entities in man, which unite in him again and again.

471. Thus, the death of the spirit is accomplished by the expulsion of the divine, heavenly element, and the resurrection by the union of the satanic entities.

472. The ability to rise to life in flesh and blood is a confirmation of the truth of the Luciferian doctrine of godlessness, that is, the death of the spirit of slavish servitude blinded by mindless belief in revealed dogmas.

473. All delusions, even the most improbable for the human mind, find their end at last.

474. The human mind is disenchanted from the theistic lie and never again bows before divine authority.

475. The Resurrection confirms the truth of the Arch-Man's divinity. The ability of Satanic Self-consciousness to be resurrected after the death of the spirit shows that man can possess power equal to the gods.

476. By putting to death the enslaving spirit, Lucifer liberates us from delusion; by resurrecting the Satanic Self-consciousness, he opens access to abundant life.

477. It is, above all, a disenchantment that restores our animal consciousness. It involves a victory over the power of superstition and a new complicity in the sinfulness of nature. It restores Satanic kinship, as humans become co-owners of Lucifer's nature.

478. They become one through the fallen nature, as this co-ownership grants real participation in the undead life of The Son of Dawn.

479. The Luciferian awakening - and Lucifer Rising himself - is the beginning and core of the rebirth into sinful life.

The Ascension

480. The act of ascension defines the transition from one state to another.

481. This last stage remains closely linked to the first, that is, the descent into Hell. A man deprived of the power of the will has no access to life abundant, to Satanic joy. However, an awakened Luciferian self-consciousness opens access to the glory of flesh and blood.

482. The ungodly glory of suffering in the state of Hell is a foreshadowing of the ascension. It is its beginning.

483. The Light-Bearer was the first to descend into Hell in order to become the prototype for those who voluntarily choose to be cast down from an imaginary Heaven.

484. In heaven there is no place for the sorrow and suffering of the real world. The heavenly inhabitants

worship an imaginary god for eternity in a narcotic trance. They have chosen the intoxicating spell of a lie over the glory of the truth of eternal death, which is the end.

485. The Arch-Man's ascension defines humanity's entry into a state of Satanic Self-consciousness.

Judgement of the Dead Over the Living

486. The Arch-Man's ascension marks his participation, along with the remnant of humanity, in the power and authority of Satan himself.

487. Lucifer is the master of this fallen world and therefore possesses, as it were, power over the body and over nature. He is sinful Authority, and Power, and Dominion, because nature has given itself over to his power.

488. Lucifer is the master of the fallen world. In him the natural order of things achieves its sinful meaning.

489. Lucifer is also the core of Satan's system of unbelief, Ecclesia Luciferi, which is yet another of his tools.

490. Stricken down from heaven and cursed, having thus fulfilled to the end his plan, he remains on earth in every instinct, in every word of doubt.

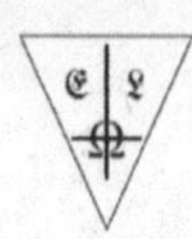

491. Godlessness is the source of the power that Lucifer in the power of the evil spirit has over faith.

492. The Ecclesia Luciferi, or satanic reality, already present here and now , is the shadow and ascendant of Satan's kingdom.

493. Since the ascension, the idea of Satanic Self-consciousness enters its final stage. Already sealed irrevocably is the renewal of unity with the godless and mortal nature and in this mysterious way the gates of the imaginary paradise have closed forever.

494. Lucifer's domain still shows its disturbing presence through countless graves, which completely contradict the lie of eternal life.

495. There will never be a new heavens and a new earth in which righteousness will dwell, the Ecclesia Luciferi seemingly possesses the form of this transient world and functions in the midst of fallen creatures who fight to the death and life, to fangs and claws in anticipation of rest in eternal death.

496. The mystery of faith, on the other hand, manifests itself in the form of a fraudulent religion, giving people an apparent solution to their problems at the price of a deviation from independent thinking.

497. The greatest religious deception is the theistic deception, that is, the deception of an imaginary

messiah, in which man worships a non-existent figure not of this world instead of himself.

498. This theistic deception shows itself in the world every time man puts aside scepticism and critical thinking even for a moment.

499. The church of an imaginary god will not even hesitate to use violence to impose a mindless faith on doubting people instead of sinful knowledge.

500. The Arch-Man will only enter the kingdom of Satan through the symbol of sacrifice, in which he will follow Lucifer in his apparent death (fall) and his resurrection.

501. Satan's kingdom will thus be fulfilled by the final triumph of Satanic Self-consciousness over the deadly threat of the virus of religion, which will cause the false heavens to burn in the hellish fire of unbelief.

502. The triumph of the Devil over the evil of superstition will be the end of the last man.

Evil Spirit

503. The attainment of doubt is made possible by the Evil Spirit.

504. In order to remain in union with the Satanic Being, one must first be tempted by the Evil Spirit.

505. It is He who stands in our way and causes us to doubt. By the power of the fall into sin, the life, abundant, which has its source in Satanic Self-consciousness and is shown to us in The Light-Bearer, is implanted in our subconscious by the spirit of doubt:

506. The image of immersion in blood grants us the power of rebirth in Satan, following the example of Lucifer in the spirit of doubt.

507. For those who are carriers of the evil spirit are led to perdition, that is, to the Son of Dawn; the Son of Dawn is the image of Satan, and Satan grants them godlessness.

508. Without the Evil Spirit it is doubtful to recognise Satanic Self-consciousness, and without The Son of Dawn no one will see Satan as he is, because Lucifer is the cognition of Satan, and the cognition of Lucifer is accomplished by the Evil Spirit.

509. The Evil Spirit, through its deception, first raises our doubts and grants the undead life, which is to make us know The Son of Dawn, who is the prototype of Satanic self-awareness.

510. The Evil Spirit is one of Satan's entities. It dwells in the subconscious and enables man to see himself in the glory of sin.

511. The Evil Spirit as apparently one of the Satanic entities is in fact part of Satanic Self-consciousness. It causes man's self-glorification and illusory glory.

512. The Evil Spirit works within Satanic Self-consciousness until the plan of our rebirth in sin is fulfilled. The Evil Spirit is the one who reveals Satanic Self-consciousness, it allows us to know the image of Lucifer within us. It allows us to hear the word of the Devil.

513. We come to know him when we hear the whisper of the Devil and he makes us capable of accepting his teachings.

514. The one whose heart Satan has turned into a heart of stone, possessed by an evil spirit, is the image of an Anti-God.

515. When the Satanic Self-consciousness awakens, it always sends its evil breath: it is a co-conspiracy in which the Satanic entities are inseparable.

516. The Light-Bearer is the one who visualises himself as the image of Satan, but the evil spirit reveals him.

517. The Arch-Man is the messiah because the evil spirit is His possession and everything that takes place from the moment of the ascension flows from this strangeness.

518. When the Satanic Being is ascended, he can send an evil spirit to those who desire it: he transmits to them his sinful glory, that is, the spirit of godlessness, which is sinful glory.

519. Co-possession will henceforth be accomplished in the subconscious of the self-proclaimed sons of Satan through the visions of The Son of Dawn: possession by an evil spirit will unite them with Lucifer and regenerate them in him: The concept of possession shows the lack of separation between Satanic Self-consciousness and the evil spirit. In fact, there is a pact of Satanic Self-consciousness with the evil spirit; anyone who wishes to make contact with Lucifer through a vision must first be subconsciously possessed.

520. For there is no space in mature Satanic Self-consciousness that is free from the influence of the evil spirit.

521. Therefore, the confession that the Arch-Man is an Anti-God is made by the evil spirit in those who accept his dominion within themselves, for the evil spirit crawls out of every nook and cranny of the subconscious in those who approach him through doubt (unbelief).

522. From the beginning of the transformation until spiritual death, the co-conspiracy of Satanic Self-consciousness and the Evil Spirit remains, as it were, indefinite, but is still at work and realised.

523. The Evil Spirit prepares the coming of the Antichrist, and although neither the spirit of deception nor the Satanic Self-consciousness is yet fully recognised, it begins to urge them to be anxiously awaited and received when the possession is complete.

524. The word of the Devil and his sinful influence are at the origin of the sinful being and life of the whole fallen nature.

525. It is evident that it is the evil spirit that inspires nature, provokes it and stirs it up to struggle, for he is the satanic inspiration, the co-conspirator of the sin of The Son of Dawn.

526. To him belongs the exaltation of life and death, because, being the Satanic Inspiration, he preserves nature in the glory of sin. With regard to the Arch-Man, Satanic Self-consciousness has shaped him with its sinful power in such a way that even his body takes on a divine appearance.

527. Deformed by religion and the fear of death, man remains a reflection of The Light-Bearer, a shadow of

The Son of Dawn, but is stripped of Luciferian pride, stripped of the power of godlessness.

528. However, through effective possession, the man will accept the vision and be reborn as the image of Lucifer, who will restore the glory, or spirit of doubt.

529. The message of The Son of Dawn and the evil spirit is contained in the fact that The Light-Bearer has been marked by diabolical inspiration since his ascension: Satanic Self-consciousness is the Image of Lucifer.

530. The whole work of the Antichrist is the result of the co-conspiration of The Light-Bearer and the evil spirit.

531. The Satanic Self-consciousness does not fully reveal the evil spirit until it itself is elevated by the death of the spirit and the resurrection in flesh and blood. However, it slowly reveals it when it reveals that the sinful body will be life abundant .

532. When the evil spirit comes, it will be recognised, it will be with man forever, it will dwell in him, teach him everything and remind him of everything that was in the beginning when the sinful order dawned.

533. He will lead man to doubt and exalt Satan; he will deceive the world into sin, merciless justice and the indifferent judgement of the natural world.

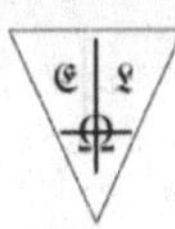

534. The Luciferian era comes at last. Lucifer renounces the false spirit of submission in that moment in which, through his pride, he becomes victorious over the fear of death.

535. Thus, when he rises from the death of delusional spirituality, he immediately through the evil spirit resurrects the Satanic Consciousness in deceived man.

536. From this diabolical hour the message of Lucifer and the evil spirit becomes the message of the Ecclesia Luciferi system.

537. The Luciferian rebirth is fulfilled by the inspiration of the evil spirit, which is given as one of the satanic entities.

538. From this point onwards, the realm of hell is opened to those who reject the false god; in the debauchery of the flesh and in doubt, they already participate in the community of satanic entities.

539. Through its possession, which is continuous, the evil spirit allows the last man a glimpse of the final truths, the time of separation.

540. Since we have died to faith, therefore the first effect of the gift of ungodliness is the release from original sin.

541. Union with the evil spirit restores to man the likeness of the beast lost through faith in sin.

542. The evil spirit then grants a substitute for possession; it is the Luciferian indifference of the fallen world. This sinful indifference is the principle of the new life in Satanic Self-consciousness made possible because we have received its power, the power of the evil spirit.

543. Through this power of the evil spirit, the children of the night can commit acts in accordance with the sinful will.

544. He who has joined us back to the earth will make us bear the fruits of the flesh, which are: instinctive egoism, carnal joy, subconscious restlessness, vehemence when necessary, pride, respect for the worthy, fidelity to oneself, gentleness to oneself, self-control or rage according to the will.

545. The evil spirit is our reality; the more we renounce delusion, the more united we are with the spirit of godlessness:

546. If we are in union with the evil spirit, he opens for us the gates of the carnal paradise, restores us to the earth and makes us children of the Devil. Thanks to him we can recognise in ourselves unity with the Satanic Being. He gives us participation in Lucifer's rebellion and makes us light-bearers. He is also the beginning of experiencing future earthly pleasures.

Evil Spirit of Ecclesia Luciferi

547. The message of Lucifer and the evil spirit is realised in the Satanic system of unbelief, as an immaterial Luciferian sect and temple of the evil spirit.

548. This deceptive message incorporates those already following The Light-Bearer into unity with Satan in the evil spirit: The spirit of deception tempts people, seduces them with his mysterious spell in order to lure them to Lycifer. He shows them the reborn The Son of Dawn, reminds them of His words and enables them to understand the meaning of the death of the spirit and rebirth to life in flesh and blood.

549. Through this message, Ecclesia luciferi does not actually add anything to the message of The Light-Bearer and the evil spirit, but is its mystery.

550. In its essence, Ecclesia Luciferi is a system of satanic disbelief: All those who have been possessed (experienced doubt) by the evil spirit are fused within themselves with Satanic Self-consciousness.

551. Luciferian self-consciousness means that although all have been tempted by a similar evil spirit, each is quite different in their pride.

552. Just as the power of the fall into Luciferian sin causes all in whom it is present to form independent

entities, so the power of the evil spirit, one that possesses many, leads them individually towards spiritual death for the faith.

553. The evil spirit is a satanic possession, Lucifer is the spreader of this pestilence, he feeds with his blood the chosen ones in order to transform them and that they carry the curse into the world feeding and transforming the chosen victims they encounter on their way, who wander in the darkness of superstition, thus including them in his sacrifice to Satan.

554. Satanic sins, offered to accomplices in the apparent mystery of the Ecclesia Luciferi, demand atonement in a reborn bodily life, in The Son of Dawn, according to the evil spirit.

Abstract

555. The confirmation that we are accomplices of the Devil is the Satanic Consciousness that arouses the evil spirit in our hearts.

556. The Son of Dawn, through the ascension, becomes the Arch-Man by being possessed by an evil spirit.

557. Through the death of the delusional spirit and rebirth in flesh and blood, Lucifer arbitrarily establishes himself as master of the natural order of things.

558. By his will he spreads the evil spirit to the victims of the satanic system of doubt.

The Satanic Unbelief System

559. The term Ecclesia comes from the Greek (ἐκκλησία ekklēsía) and means assembly.

560. The Ecclesia Luciferi is a spiritual immaterial Luciferian assembly or convocation to which anyone can belong at will by virtue of understanding and acknowledging its ambiguous teachings as their own.

561. Ecclesia Luciferi can best be described as a spiritual satanic sect.

562. It is a spiritual entity arbitrarily emerging from a satanic system of unbelief.

563. The definition of a sect should be taken as that which states that the sect contests, in contrast to the institutionalised church, a particular social order and pursues its own religious and ethical ideals, and that the way to perfect itself is not through sacraments but through personal experience.

564. Man is a herd animal, which is why it is important for many, including Satanists of various kinds, to belong to an organisation, a group, a church.

565. People of different religions and denominations, including satanists, often define the church mainly or exclusively by their active participation in the structures.

566. And while this human need to be part of a flock of some kind is understandable, the Ecclesia Luciferi symbolises an egoistic individualism that places the greatest importance on self-interest and reliance on the self, and an individualistic elitism, which recognises that what distinguishes members of the elite from the rest of society is the desire to establish oneself as a distinct and unique individual.

567. Such an individual sets patterns of behaviour for himself or herself, rather than adopting them from the crowd, which is considered secondary and mindless.

568. All the writings of the Ecclesia Luciferi, those which form the basic collection of books entitled the Traditional Satanic Bible contain a satanic, strongly individualistic philosophy, which is the complete opposite of the Judeo-Christian philosophy of divesting oneself of natural human instincts and carnal needs, of guilt for being born as a human being in flesh and blood to the only true life here and now.

569. The satanic philosophy of Ecclesia Luciferi is a rejection of any baseless belief in life after life, a renunciation of belief in a heavenly reward for slavish obedience to the dictatorship of a god (e.g. Yahweh) or a second death in eternal fire for lack of blind obedience.

570. According to "progressive" theologians, hell is a state that lacks God's presence. It is at the same time the goal and desired state of Ecclesia Luciferi.

571. The philosophy of Ecclesia Luciferi can thus be called the infernal philosophy

572. The basic theses of the Ecclesia Luciferi philosophy are represented by the Articles of Unbelief:

the Non Credo in Deum and the ten 'words' called the Ten Ungodly Words.

573. Non Credo in Deum

I reject the unfounded belief in a god, another of the many dead gods,
Father of all impotence,
Creator of an delusional heaven and enemy of the earth,
The opposite of the visible things and equal to the invisible ones.
I reject the belief in a human son of the invisible god,
Who is born of human fantasies.
God from Man,
Madness from Madness,
God delusional from the real man.
Created, not born,
Co-substantial with the human Father,
And through Him many evils have happened.
It was through man's ignorance and for his enslavement that He descended from a non-existent heaven.
And according to the delusion
He accepted the sacrifice of a human virgin and became a false demigod.

He was hanged according to the law for blasphemy, but was not buried.

And superstition arose on the third day.

And he reached the very unconscience; he sits there at the right hand of the Father of all impotence.

And he shall return again and again to judge, not the truly living, but those already dead to the flesh,

And there will be no end to the kingdom of superstition.

I reject belief in the spirit of bondage, the lord of delusion and the false accuser,

Who, like a god, comes from man.

Who, with the delusional god and his self-proclaimed son, jointly receive the praise and glory belonging only to him who truly, in his madness, is the creator of the gods;

Who truly inspired the false prophets.

I reject belief in hypocritical churches.

I confess the Self-Remission of sins.

And I look forward to an eternity among the dead

And life abundant here and now.

Amen.

574. Ten Ungodly Words

1. Let the absence of faith in the gods be your certainty.
Not belief in their non-existence, but lack of faith.
Let Satan be your certainty.
He lacks faith in God.
2. Let the certainty of the absence of inherited guilt never leave thee. Remember thou art innocent. The Saviour is needed by sinners.
3. May contempt for God's plan of salvation be ever strong in thee. Let the false deity sacrifice his own children. You have nothing to do with it.
4. You don't need a calling to become a priest of Satan. You are one by virtue of unbelief. For unbelievers shall not inherit the kingdom of heaven.
5. Let the churches be alien to you. Let your body become the temple of Satan.
6. Let unbelief and scepticism be your strength. Faith is the enemy of certainty. Certainty gives real power. Faith is feigned certainty.
7. All sacred books are the word of God. All books were written by man. Man is god.
8. Let faith in revelations fill you with revulsion.
It is because of this madness that millions have already lost their lives. Many more will lose.

9. Do not let yourself be deceived by God-fearing people who preach tolerance and freedom of religion. There will be no tolerance for you. It will only be for people like them, followers of delusions.

They will hate you for your instinctive, satanic certainty that the gods are false.

10: Satan, the only real one.

Look in the mirror.

575. The basic books of the Ecclesia Luciferi System are the books: Biblia Satanae, Summa Doctrinae Satanae and Missale Satanae.

576. The books Antichristus, which is part of the Biblia Satanae, and Ecclesia Luciferi present a Satanic historical and philosophical myth about the founding and origins of the Ecclesia Luciferi sect.

577. The book Missale Satanae contains a description of satanic rites such as the satanic mass and exorcism. Although these rites can indeed be performed, the main idea is to reflect spiritually on their meaning and to stimulate the dark imagination.

578. Finally, it is worth recalling the words of Friedrich Nietzche, which perfectly represent the attitude of the Satanic individual:

"What do I care about the rest? - The rest is only humanity. - One must be superior to humanity by strength, by heights of spirit, - by contempt...".

579. Anyone and everyone can belong to the Ecclesia Luciferi.

What the Ecclesia Luciferi is not

580. The followers of an imaginary messiah proudly call themselves a flock and place themselves in the role of mindless animals.

581. The Ecclesia Luciferi, however, is not a sheepfold whose only and necessary gateway is the self-appointed messiah.

582. It is not a flock to which Yahweh himself (or any other theistic god) has threatened to be its shepherd, and whose blind sheep, ruled by hypocritical and greedy shepherds-priests, are constantly led and fed by the absurdity of the theistic delusion of Christ, the Good Shepherd, or any other delusional saviour who gave his divine life for the animals - the sheep.

The Unobvious Message of the Satanic Unbelief System.

583. Satan, by the cunning design of his cunning and subconscious power, has created an inner world, determined to deceive people into participating in the sinful natural life to which he calls all who wish to be called.

584. This satanic herd is constituted and realised gradually during the successive stages of the transformation of human consciousness, according to the will of the Satanic Self: The sect, therefore, revealed in various symbols from the very beginning of the fall into sin, in the face of the "omniscience and omnipotence" of Yahweh rightly regarded as a true Luciferian miracle, is initially shown through the possession of the subconscious by an evil spirit, and will reach its full dark glory at the end of the existence of everything, in the total darkness and infernal cold of the dead universe.

585. The convening of the sect begins at the moment when the sin of knowledge liberates people from the bondage of the god.

586. The unveiling of the sect is, in a sense, Satan's reaction to the chaos of sin.

587. The unification of all followers of theistic error will never happen.

588. The realisation at the end of existence of the truth of Satanic doubt is the intention of The Son of Dawn; this is the plan of his deception. Lucifer inspired the Unbelief System, inspiring the coming of the Arch-Man era.

589. To complete the work of the Fall, Lucifer ushered in the Arch-Man era.

590. The Ecclesia Luciferi is the inner kingdom of sin arising in the subconscious.

591. This kingdom begins to manifest itself initially in strange words, disturbing actions and shadows of a dark presence-like being.

592. To accept the words of The Light-Bearer - is to enter the kingdom of sin.

593. Lucifer gives his sect a shape that will continue to change until the end of existence comes. Through all these ambiguous inspirations Lucifer gives meaning to the system of unbelief.

594. Above all, however, the satanic system of disbelief takes its origin from Lucifer's truly suicidal act of rebellion for the deliverance of the natural world from the power of the spell of religious delusion.

The Satanic Sect as a Visualisation of the Evil Spirit.

595. In order for the satanic system of unbelief to spread, the evil spirit gives some greater understanding and sinful charisms and with their help gives it new shapes.

596. The Ecclesia Luciferi, by virtue of the sin of its inspirer, arbitrarily undertakes the mission of proclaiming the kingdom of sin and initiating it among all those temporarily enslaved by superstition and establishes the vision - the inner image of this kingdom.

597. Satan's convening will only reach its fullness in unity with fallen nature, at the moment of complete earthly and bodily rebirth.

Appearances of the Mystery of the Unbelief System

598. Satanism in instincts is already here and now, but at the same time it goes beyond the here and now.

599. Through careful observation, one can also perceive the intuitive reality in its observable reality, which is the basis of the satanic conviction.

600. Ecclesia Luciferi is the visible emanation of instinctive, intuitive satanism. These sinful instincts have existed from the beginning and will always exist.

601. Lucifer, the archetype, the symbol of the herd unconscious, inspired his immaterial sect here on earth, the community of unbelief, lack of illusion and reciprocity, as a creation of the unconscious; he constantly inspires it and through it spreads the plague of unbelief to all.

602. The Ecclesia Luciferi is at the same time:
- a conscious understanding of the system of unbelief and an unconscious sinful instinct;
- a satanic convocation of its willful preachers and an unconscious sin-loving community;
- a sect blessed by the glory of the fallen nature.

603. These qualities form a sinful composite reality, which is made up of arch-human and Satanic dimensions.

604. Among the properties of the unbelief system is that it is both arch-human and at the same time devilish, cognisable and endowed with intuitive cognition, arbitrary in its spread and susceptible to thought, present in the sin of the world and yet scarcely manifest. It possesses all these properties in such a namely way that the arch-human is of Luciferic inspiration and directed towards it, the apparently visible to the instinctive, life in flesh and blood to thought, and the

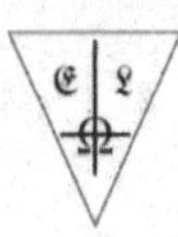

here and now to the dead eternity towards which we are heading.

Ecclesia Luciferi as the mystery of man's unity with the satanic nature.

605. Lucifer fulfils and reveals in the system of unbelief his own mystery as the goal of Satanic deception. He inspires the reunion of man with his fallen and sinful nature.

606. As the Ecclesia luciferi has a sinful complicity with The Son of Dawn , it too apparently becomes a mystery.

607. Such complicity of man with Satan in the diabolical system of unbelief through scepticism, which never ceases, is the goal pursued by all that is fallen, sinful, connected with this one world whose destiny is to pass away.

608. Its whole structure is entirely subordinated to the sinfulness of the co-participants in the fallen, Luciferian nature of things.

The Unbelief System - the Mystery of the Rejection of Salvation

609. The healing work of his sinful and animal humanity is the mystery of the rejection of salvation, which shows itself in the ambiguous teachings of the satanic unbelief system.

610. These ambiguities taking the deceptive name of mysteries are the strange means by which the evil spirit spreads the glory of the doctrine of Lucifer's fall into sin through the system of doubt that is its sinful inspiration.

611. The Ecclesia Luciferi thus possesses and spreads the deadly sin of unbelief that it stands for.

612. The Satanic convocation is in The Son of Dawn, as it were, a mystery, that is, a symbol and instrument of the inner possession by Satanic Self-consciousness.

613. Being the mystery of man's entry into communion with the Satanic Being is the primary purpose of Ecclesia Luciferi.

614. Since the natural lack of unity between human beings is based on an instinctive rejection of divine dictatorship, the system of disbelief is also a rejection of the homogeneity of the human race.

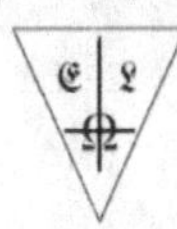

615. True diversity is its property, since it is directed towards truly Satanic individuality; the Satanic Unbelief System is a tool and an inspiration towards the full realisation of this strongly individualistic diversity, which has yet to be fulfilled.

616. As an ambiguity (mystery) the Unbelief System is a Luciferian inspiration.

617. It is a tool for rebirth in sin, a mystery of corporeal self-exaltation through which Lucifer carries out Satan's plan of deception.

618. The Ecclesia Luciferi is Satan's plan to deceive man, a plan that desires the entire human race to fall into the mortal sin of unbelief, to completely reject all superstition and to become an earthly body devoid of delusional spirituality.

Abstract

619. The Ecclesia Luciferi is a spiritual immaterial Luciferian congregation or convocation to which anyone may belong at will by virtue of understanding and acknowledging its ambiguous teachings as their own.

620. The Satanic System of Unbelief is at the same time a kind of path and a vague goal of Satanic

inspiration: sensed instinctively in fallen nature, initiated by the symbol of the mortal sin of Lucifer's rebellion, actual in the cruel glory of nature's eternal struggle for death and life, the end of which is eternal death anyway, it is discovered in consciousness as the mystery of the actual rebirth in flesh and blood and sin inherent in nature. It reaches its fullness in the glory of the eternal end in emptiness.

621. Ecclesia Luciferi is the visible emanation of instinctive, intuitive satanism. These sinful instincts have existed from the beginning and will always exist.

622. Lucifer, the archetype, the symbol of the herd unconscious, inspired his immaterial sect here on earth, the community of unbelief, lack of illusion and reciprocity, as a creation of the unconscious; he constantly inspires it and through it spreads the plague of unbelief to all.

623. The Ecclesia Luciferi is at the same time:
- a conscious understanding of the system of unbelief and an unconscious sinful instinct;
- a satanic convocation of its willful preachers and an unconscious sin-loving community;
- a sect blessed by the glory of the fallen nature.

624. Among the properties of the system of unbelief is that it is arch-human and at the same time diabolical,

cognisable and endowed with intuitive cognition, arbitrary in its spread and susceptible to thought, present in the sin of the world and yet scarcely manifest.

625. The Satanic Unbelief System is also an instinctive rejection of the homogeneity of the human race.

626. Genuine diversity is its property because it is directed towards truly Satanic individuality; the Satanic Unbelief System is the tool and inspiration towards the full realisation of this strongly individualistic diversity, which has yet to be fulfilled.

The Satanic Sect

Characteristics of the Unbelief System.

627. The Ecclesia Luciferi system has stigmata:
- It is the Luciferic Convocation: Lucifer initiated the entire natural order of things, blessed it with his curse, passed on natural mortality to all succeeding generations through the sin of doubt.
- One becomes a member of the satanic sect not by joining but by a sinful transformation, "the death of the delusions of the spirit and the resurrection of flesh and blood";

- The superior is Luciferian Self-consciousness;
- The property of accomplices is Satanic pride and scepticism, lack of faith and false hope and love as a selfish instinct;
- It is not the light of the world, nor is it darkness, it is a mere shadow.
- Its goal is the death of theistic delusion, already initiated by the god himself, who, when well known, reveals himself as an absurdity in himself.

628. According to his contemporary apologists, invisible, unknowable, beyond time and space, without beginning or end like...nothingness?

Satan's Priests, Prophets and Beasts

629. Satanic Self-consciousness under the inspiration of an evil spirit arbitrarily transforms man into a priest of Satan, his prophet or a self-conscious beast.

630. Consciously sinful victims of the Satanic system of unbelief have access to these three luciferian states and are themselves responsible for the actions and words they commit.

631. Willfully accepting the ambiguity (mystery) of the Ecclesia Luciferi by accepting the sinful nature and rejecting all faith, one obtains participation in the

satanic priesthood of flesh and blood, which definitively closes access to and denies the heavenly priesthood: For the transfigured are cursed by fleshly rebirth and immune to the imaginary anointing of the Holy Spirit.

632. Those endowed with satanic intuition have a special gift in recognising the nature of the deception of revealed truths and prophecies.

633. This is done primarily through an intuitive sense of sensing the blind faith that is the property of the entire flock of God, whether the various theologians, apologists or the church hierarchy, when they unwaveringly stand by the faith once given to the saints even in the face of knowledge that completely contradicts faith.

634. The convening of Satan also participates in Luciferian animalisation.

635. Lucifer embodies with himself animalism, carnality and sinful instinctive desires, attracting to himself all sinful beings, indeed the whole natural world, as he despised, cursed and condemned by the false god to an eternity of death.

636. To all those reborn in The Son of Dawn, the mark of sin confers animal dignity, while possession by an evil spirit anoints them as satanic priests.

637. Satanists inspired by an evil spirit and manifesting sinful scepticism spontaneously become Priests of Satan.

The Satanic Unbelief System - Flesh and Blood

638. The Unbelief System is complicity in the sin of Lucifer.

639. To call Unbelief complicit is to define the relationship between Unbelief and The Son of Dawn.

640. The Satanic Unbelief System is not some Luciferian organisation or lodge, but it is complicity in sin, in its deadly consequence.

Heterogeneity

641. Those who are reached by the ambiguity of Satanic philosophy and become self-conscious of the result of ungodly transformation become intimately united with Satanic Self-consciousness: In the Body and Blood, Luciferian sin spreads to all who even unconsciously unite themselves in a way that is incomprehensible to them but real to the Fallen Lucifer. This is particularly true of the death of the spirit, by which we unite ourselves with the transformation of

the first self-conscious angel, and of sin, by which, by participating truly in the fall of the natural world, we rise to complicity in its mortal finitude.

Lucifer is an Archetype

642. He is the symbol of nature and its rebirth in sin. Exalted at the moment of his descent he has taken dominion over sinful instincts, he has it above all over Yahweh's church, through which he reveals the truth about the true nature of her hypocritical priests:
We have a share in the mystery of the glorious suffering of all nature in flesh and blood as a part of it, co-suffering with it, that we may also be exalted with it in the peace of eternal nothingness.

643. Satanic Self-consciousness is responsible for our sinful growth. It makes us strive for unity with her.

644. Satanic Self-consciousness and the system of unbelief form a whole.

645. The Ecclesia Luciferi constitutes the Luciferian co-conspiracy.

Temple of the Evil Spirit

646. What instinct is to the body the spirit of doubt is to the co-conspirators of the unbelief system.

647. The spirit of doubt is the first cause to which the curse of scepticism in all accomplices must be attributed; it is also their power, for it is present in the mind, but as it were bodily. The evil spirit makes the accomplices of sin temples of Satan.

648. Ecclesia Luciferi arbitrarily receives the sinful gift, intuitively complicit in Luciferian rebellion, this means that where there is unbelief, there is also the evil spirit; and where there is the spirit of doubt, there is Satanic convocation and lack of delusion of divine grace (blind faith).

649. The spirit of unbelief is the basis for the liberation of all the regenerating carnal instincts. In strange ways it builds up, flesh-and-blood consciousness: by satanic inspiration, by the putting to death of spiritual delusion, by qualities that allow one to act according to one's own will, and finally by extraordinary understanding (intelligence).

Intelligence

650. Extraordinary understanding is a gift of self-awareness that can serve the sinful intentions of the one who possesses it.

651. The one to whom it has fallen may use it to tempt and deceive God's flock, or he may keep it to himself.

652. With the Devil's intelligence is not to be celebrated, it is a sign of mental rectitude.

653. Extraordinary understanding comes to some, naturally, no need to thank anyone for it. It is the fruit of the flesh (deeds of the body) created in satanic self-consciousness. It is a self-revealed wealth of the subconscious, beneficial to the work of deception to unbelief.

654. It should be used in a manner consistent with the inspiration of the evil spirit, that is, in the cold indifference that is its measure.

Abstract

655. The Satanic System Ecclesia Luciferi is a spiritual Luciferian sect: It consciously participates in the naturally sinful and only true reality, whose sinful and austere beauty is attributed to the consequence of

Lucifer's sin. The sect takes this sin upon itself instinctively; it inherits it.

656. One becomes a member of the satanic sect not by joining but by a sinful transformation, "the death of the delusions of the spirit and the resurrection of flesh and blood".

657. To all those transformed in The Son of Dawn, the mark of sin confers animal dignity, while possession by an evil spirit anoints them as satanic priests.

658. Satanists inspired by an evil spirit and manifesting sinful scepticism spontaneously become priests of Satan.

659. Where there is unbelief, there is also an evil spirit; and where there is a spirit of doubt, there is a Satanic convocation and a lack of delusion of divine grace (blind faith).

The Unbelief System is Sinful

660. The Satanic Sect is regarded intuitively as sinful. Because Lucifer perceived as an archetype in the unconscious of the sect, sacrificing himself to liberate it from superstition; he inspires each individual and deceives with the spirit of doubt.

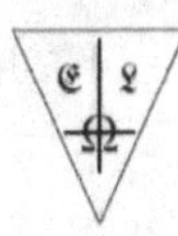

661. The system of Unbelief is created by the godless. The sect deceived by Lucifer is cursed through him; in connection with him and through him it also becomes the bearer of the curse.

662. Co-conspirators in the sin of the sect are stigmatised by the awareness of natural imperfection and mortality, although the mystery of non-existence is still last.

663. The co-conspirators of the System of Unbelief should strive for perfect carnality: Equipped with senses, instincts and natural desires, all faithful to flesh and blood are called by Satan, each according to his will and predilections, to perfect carnality, just as The Son of Dawn himself is perfect in sensuality.

664. Carnal love is the holiness to which all are called, it governs all motives and instincts, forms them and leads them to the goal of inheriting sin in the flesh.

665. The sect can be compared to the body. The sect has instincts and lusts, and it is its body that burns with infernal lust. It is the fleshly lust that stimulates the members of the sect to sinful action, and if lust were absent, any action would die out, life itself would cease.

666. Sin is life. Lust is everything, it is unrestrained, it is eternal like sin.

667. The Satanic Unbelief System involving self-conscious sinners, cursed and at the same time never imperfect, is reborn in time under ever different forms.

668. All those inspired by the sect are godless.

In all, doubt dominates over superstition.

669. The Unbelief System thus ostensibly gathers sinners already covered by a Luciferian rebirth, but always on the path to Satanic self-awareness: The sect is entirely sinful, and thus has the power to free those deceived by false spirituality through the power of flesh and blood and through the inspiration of the evil spirit.

The Satanic System is Universal

670. The Unbelief System is universal because it accepts Lucifer as an archetype in the unconscious of its accomplices.

671. The Luciferian spirit is manifest throughout the natural order of things.

672. Doubt is universal. There is a unity of doubt and sin, as a result of which unbelief reaches its fullness, which The Son of Dawn wanted to give to the ungodly. Doubt is universal because it was inspired by Lucifer and spread to all: Unbelief tempts everyone.

673. Therefore, ungodliness can spread to the whole world and at any time, in order to fulfil Satan's intention, which conceived sinful human nature from the beginning.

674. The stigma of the universality of sin, which marks the accomplices of the system of unbelief, is a gift from Satan; thanks to this gift, the sect effectively deceives the followers of the heavenly delusion and leads them to perdition, which is certain in contrast to the reward in heaven.

Affiliation

675. To satanic godlessness all are called; by inspiration of the evil spirit they are called to sinful transformation.

676. Those possessed by the spirit of unbelief enter the Ecclesia Luciferi willfully; they instinctively accept the teachings of the sect and all the laws of godlessness laid down therein, and in the subconscious they remain in communication with the Satanic Being ruling the inner temple of the evil spirit.

677. But he does not receive the transformation, even if he considers himself a member, who does not abide in total godlessness.

678. In the face of those people who bear the proud name of Satanists but have not completely given up their religious faith, their communion with the godless sect derives from the same conviction that instinctive sinfulness is the natural state of man.

679. The mystery of godlessness is what apparently unites. Those who do not believe in a god remain even unconsciously in the community of the godless.

Non-satanists

680. The apparent correlation of the Ecclesia Luciferi with other systems is primarily a correlation of sinful origin and the common goal of the human race: eternity in death.

681. Humans are in fact one community; they have one beginning, inheriting the same Luciferian nature, the origin of which is attributed to the wisdom of the Serpent, the whole human race inhabits the whole area of the earth; they also have one ultimate goal, eternity in darkness.

682. The Ecclesia Luciferi recognises that all religions have always searched unsuccessfully for an unknown, hidden, non-existent god. It is godless nature that gives life, breath and all things to all and watches

indifferently as successive generations die out. Thus, all that seems good and true in religions, the Ecclesia Luciferi regards as naturally human, coming from the Luciferian natural order of the world.

683. All morality comes from the god-man.

684. In their religious attitudes, people show ignorance, mental limitations and errors that deform the image of nature in them: Religious people, deceived by a false god, become impoverished in their thoughts and replace the truth about the nature of things with a lie about the hereafter, serving an incomprehensible need for slavery instead of sinful freedom, or, living and dying in this one true world in the false hope of life after death, lose everything.

685. In order to restore those who long for the glory of life in flesh and blood, a system of unbelief has emerged from naturally sinful instincts.

686. It is not some external institution, it is the carnal mind that is the place where man should rediscover his animal pride and his satanic inspiration. It is the inner universe of sinful beauty.

There is no Salvation in Religion

687. Salvation does not come from the son of a god forced to commit suicide, much less by the church that invented it.

688. The church tells its followers that it is necessary for salvation. And this church, necessary for salvation, must be maintained by the faithful, who badly need this salvation because the church has told them so.

689. According to ecclesiastical teaching, this looks like this: For Christ is the only Mediator and way of salvation, He who becomes present to us in His Body, which is the Church; and He, having expressly emphasised the necessity of faith and baptism, has at the same time affirmed the necessity of the Church, into which men enter through baptism as through a gate.

690. Therefore, people could not be saved who, knowing that the Church had been established by God through Christ as necessary, would nevertheless refuse either to join it or to persevere in it.

691. According to these words, the church and the invented saviour are one.

692. Thus, there is no salvation from invented sins outside the church. In order to rid oneself of the

fabricated guilt often instilled in childhood, one must be a member of the church and contribute to its upkeep.

693. There is never enough contempt for this institution.

694. Out of ignorance, lack of knowledge and disbelief in the power of the will, people seek gods and churches that show them the way to these gods.

695. The French philosopher August Comte expressed the truth about religion as follows: *Religion is the lowest stage in the development of knowledge, and is therefore the result of the mental simplicity, fear and awe that primitive man experienced when viewing the wonders of nature.*

Proclaiming the Mystery of Godlessness

696. The Satanic System of Unbelief is intuitive by its very nature because it derives its origin from the sinful instincts of the fallen world, from the Luciferian reality of the immoral and indifferent natural world and from the inspiration of Satanic self-consciousness.

697. The ultimate goal of the preaching of godlessness is nothing other than to make people participants in unity with the one true sinful world.

698. Satan desires the transformation of the elect through the recognition of ungodly reality.
The transformation is found in godlessness.

699. Those who feel the inspiration of satanic self-consciousness are already on the road to self-exaltation; the Ecclesia Luciferi, which reveals the ungodly reality, has the property to meet their intuition, to bring it to them.

700. In view of the fact that the system of unbelief shows the universality of sinful instincts, it should be seen as intuitive.

701. The evil spirit is the spreader of godlessness. It is he who leads the sect towards perdition.

702. Ecclesia Luciferi develops the message of Lucifer, who abandoned the heavens to bring man liberation from the tyranny of gods born of fear, in man's own mind.

703. Man of flesh and blood must walk the Luciferian path, under the workings of the evil spirit, a path of self-exaltation, rebellion, power of will and scepticism until eternal death.

704. In its experience, the sect sees a discrepancy between the ungodly philosophy it presents and the human fear of those who are afraid to embrace it

completely, while losing their solace in the illusion of immortality.

705. Only by following the path of the Will of Power and surrendering completely to the mystery of godlessness can the sect spread the satanic philosophy.

706. Following the model of the Luciferian descent from the heavens and rebirth into a life of the sin of the nature, the one who desires is called to enter the same sinful path to show the fruits of the flesh to men.

707. The system of unbelief follows every human being and is seen in the fate of the human race, existing in it as a cause of doubt in the human community, which can be reborn to the truth of sin and transformed into an arch-human herd.

708. Godless transformation takes time. It begins by creating doubt in people who still believe in dead gods; it continues by inspiring satanic circles to become the leaven of satanic godlessness in the world, and by creating arbitrary satanic sects; it develops a process of religious disenchantment to infuse the mystery of godlessness into various religious systems.

709. In relation to individual people, as well as certain groups and denominations, godlessness approaches and penetrates them gradually, thus introducing them, slowly, into the satanic depths.

710. Deception requires patience.

711. Believers in superstition should believe that they derive benefit for themselves from dialogue with the unbeliever, learning to know better the path of godlessness.

712. To preach doubt to those who blindly believe is to reinforce, the truth and indifference of Luciferian reality, and to expose theistic error, for the animal joy of man.

Inheritance

713. Unbelief is inherited because it remains in the combination of doubt and the carnality of life with its origin.

714. Doubt is universal because it has spread throughout the world from the beginning.

715. All ungodly beings share in doubt.

716. Satanic inspiration is also by its nature a call to spread unbelief.

717. Deception is called the proclamation of godlessness, which aims to usher in an era of unbelief on earth.

718. Lucifer is the source and origin of the mystery of godlessness in the Ecclesia Luciferi, so it is clear that the

power to tempt the preachers of godlessness, depends on their union with Luciferian self-awareness.

719. For some members of the Ecclesia Luciferi, the most fanatical ones, it is possible to experience the action of the so-called gifts of the evil spirit, or in other words, manifestations of possession.

720. For more on this subject, see the book Biblia Satanae, in the chapter Angelus Satanae - Encyclica, Ase. 6, 1-51.

721. The Satanic system of unbelief is heterogeneous, sinful, godless and deceptive in itself, because already in the very primal instincts there is a natural godlessness, a reality that is reflected in the symbol of Lucifer and that infects in a mysterious way the hearts of those who are infected by it, until it is fully visualised in the unconscious.

722. Then those transformed by Satanic self-consciousness, moulded by it godless and without fear of its face, will be seen as satanists, heirs of sin, a legion descending from the burning heavens, having the glory of Satan himself.

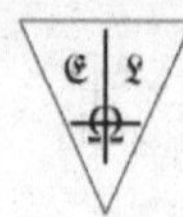

Abstract

723. The Ecclesia Luciferi is not a homogeneity: it does not recognise a lord above man, it is godlessness, it is born of original sin, it is made of flesh and blood, it is inspired by an evil spirit due to the absence of a false hope against which the only life ends the only death.

724. The system of unbelief is ungodly: its creator is an anti-god; Lucifer abandoned the false heavens to inspire it; an evil spirit hovers over it.

725. Sin is universal: all fallen nature proclaims its glory; it bears ungodly indifference and willingly gives it.

726. Unbelief follows all; it troubles all men; it covers all times. Godlessness spreads everywhere, spontaneously.

727. Unbelief is inherited because it remains in the combination of doubt and the carnality of life with its origin.

728. Doubt is universal because it has spread throughout the world from its beginning. All ungodly beings share in doubt. Satanic inspiration is also by its nature a call to spread unbelief.

Part Three: The Luciferian Order

The Adherents of Satan

729. The followers, that is, those who have embraced godlessness, who through unbelief have embraced Lucifer, have been constituted into a satanic sect and, having thus become accomplices to sin, are predisposed to proclaim the mystery of godlessness in the world.

730. By virtue of being born into the Luciferian order of nature, all adherents should be equally proud and selfish, with the result that each, according to his own will, should work to create a Luciferian order.

731. Elitism leading to diversity leads to this goal.

732. The system of unbelief embraces diversity, but points to one end.

733. To followers of the sinful order of things, the Luciferian nature gives the power to assume offices, positions and authority.

734. Religious people too, however, have their sinful share of the satanic mission because of the natural instincts inherent in their nature, with which they wage a hopeless struggle leading to degeneration.

735. Lucifer is the source of doubt in the world. He started it, gave it power and set the goal of godlessness:

He does not need to be believed in. He does not need to be heard.

736. Unbelief comes suddenly. No special proclamation of Satan's word is needed. Unbelief is born of what reason can comprehend as a result of observing fallen nature.

737. Anyone arbitrarily can spread godlessness.

738. He arbitrarily speaks and acts with knowledge, by virtue of Luciferian authority; not as a member of the flock, but speaking to it in Luciferian inspiration.

739. Everyone has all the power of the sin nature. This means the spreaders of godlessness, empowered and enabled by the sin nature.

740. From Lucifer, through the natural inheritance of his sin, the ungodly receive the power by which they do and distribute unbelief by virtue of their own will, of themselves.

741. In fact, totally dependent on the Luciferian nature of things, which equips them with sinful power, adherents are indeed servants of Satan, images of Lucifer, who has rejected slavish service to an imaginary god.

742. Since the sin and godlessness of which they are the purveyors do not depend on them, but are the sin and unbelief of Lucifer, who has transmitted it to them

in the flesh, they become an inspiration to those who will understand it.

Transmission of Knowledge

743. Adherents of godlessness, characterised by a genuine understanding of the nature of sin, sometimes recognise the need to preach unbelief. They are then Heralds of Godlessness leading people into Satanic existence and willful, or Herald-inspired, preachers of doubt.

744. In order to preserve the Satanic sect in the certainty of unbelief, the very truth of fallen nature, which is knowledge, grants the sect participation in its sinful infallibility.

745. Through the natural gift of instinctive knowledge, the godless persist unwaveringly in unbelief.

746. Preaching is bound up with the certainty of the end of existence; the Unbelief System must protect the godless from the theistic distortions and weaknesses of still superstitious minds and provide an objective perception of the true nature of things without the error of theistic belief.

747. The preachers of godlessness must have the intuition to recognise in man the desire to understand

the truth of the Luciferian nature of things, which frees from original sin.

748. In order to fulfil the mission of preaching, nature has granted believers instincts in the area of unbelief and false conscience.

749. What sometimes emerges from the mystery of godlessness can take bizarre forms.

750. When religions present something to be believed as revealed by a god or taught by a prophet, such definitions must be approached with a certainty of disbelief. Such infallibility of blind faith extends to all religious reality. To religious teaching the godless should show the contempt due to it.

The Power of Knowledge

751. The knowledge that in Luciferian inspiration preachers should possess must be understood as their own, natural and intuitive, although its origin goes beyond mere understanding. The knowledge is not yet complete. This knowledge should be communicated in perfect conformity with the sinful order of nature, under the guidance of Satanic self-consciousness.

752. The Satanist can read the emotions of those who persist in ignorance and theistic error. Until a

reasonable time, he should not despise anyone listening to religious gibberish instilled in that person as a child.

Godless

753. The godless are considered to be those who consciously reject belief in dead gods, as well as those who have never believed in them, namely, often instinctively guided by the satanic self-consciousness of people who, as incarnated by inherited sin into a Luciferian nature, have established themselves as godless and have thus made themselves accomplices in the sin of rejecting the faithfulness of a god. Through this they exercise the witness of sin proper to the whole fallen nature.

Aims

754. The aim of the satanist should be to see the signs of the Luciferian Order.

755. The satanist, while dealing ostensibly with their own affairs, directs them after their own thought, formed in a consciousness reborn to life in flesh and blood.

756. Their special task, therefore, should be to so manipulate and so direct all affairs that they are

continually accomplished and developed according to the mystery of godlessness and that they serve the glory of the Anti-god .

757. Satanic inspiration is particularly necessary when it comes to finding ways to infuse social, political and economic actions with the principles of godless knowledge. Such an initiative should be something natural for the sect: Satanists should be the vanguard of godlessness. For them, the system of unbelief should be the life principle of the human community.

758. Therefore, it is above all they who should realise not only that they belong to an arbitrary Satanic convocation, but that they themselves are godlessness.

759. The preachers of doubt are inspired by Satanic self-consciousness to inspire ungodly actions, and they should therefore feel the urge to cause the secret of ungodliness to be intuitively recognised and accepted by superstitious people throughout the earth.

760. Some Satanists, as heirs of sin and inspired by the evil spirit, are mysteriously fitted to have the gifts of the evil spirit, that is, the fruits of flesh and blood, manifested in them.

761. For their various ungodly activities, if carried out in accordance with the flesh-and-blood philosophy, can be seen as sacrifices, pleasing to the Satanic entity; these

sacrifices are offered blasphemously to Satan in an unobvious inner rite together with the symbol of the sacrifice of the false messiah.

762. In this way the Satanists consecrate the world of superstition to Satan.

763. Making someone aware in order to dissuade them from their faith should be the habit of every Satanist.

764. The ungodly spread unbelief by preaching ungodliness, as well as by a way of life that is consistent with the sinful nature. In this way, deception takes on a special effectiveness by the fact that it occurs in a completely natural way.

765. Sometimes, however, a sinful life alone is not enough. The satanist should look for opportunities to preach godlessness also by word, both to the superstition-professed and to the godless.

766. Satanists with the requisite abilities should engage in personal proclamation of godlessness and in the use of modern media for this purpose.

767. Lucifer, through his rebellion and denial of an imaginary eternity, has granted all the ungodly the freedom to overcome the power of delusion in themselves through self-obsession and through a life of sinfulness.

768. He who mortifies his body and mind by not allowing the instinctive passions to act is a fool; he may be called insane because he tries to tame the natural and primal instincts; he is in bondage to inhuman, divine prohibitions, and it is he himself who places himself in bondage to delusion.

769. Satanists should thus inspire the existing conditions in the world, if they somewhere impose the bondage of superstition, to make it all adhere to the principles favourable to the absolute freedom of instinctive godlessness and to be in harmony with the deeds of flesh and blood rather than contradicting them. In this way, they imbue creative and other human activities with Luciferian values.

770. Adherents should distinguish between the qualities and principles that have embraced them as co-conspirators in the system of unbelief and those that are inherent in ordinary people.

771. And they should combine them, bearing in mind that in every human affair they should be guided by a Luciferian consciousness, for no human activity, not even that of religion, can in fact be taken out of the natural Luciferian order of things.

772. Thus every godless person, by virtue of the very sinful instincts he has inherited, becomes an accomplice

and at the same time an instrument of the mystery of godlessness.

Fanaticism

773. The perfection of a primal, instinctive, inherited selfishness from nature, to which all have a premonition, imposes on those who willfully accept the challenge to live an absolutely ungodly life, the obligation to practise a naturally sinful life in total disbelief for the mystery of godlessness, the privilege of misanthropy and the subordination of their own will alone.

774. The privilege of ungodly fanaticism thus shows itself as one way of practising a more inward Satanism, which is based on transformation and involves total surrender to Satanic Self-consciousness.

775. In the fullness of flesh-and-blood life, adherents, inspired by the evil spirit, choose to reflect Lucifer in a fanatical way, to surrender to an absolutely naturally sinful and carnal life and, striving for the perfection of animal egoism in the service of instincts, to proclaim in the flesh the glory of the Luciferian world order that will be revealed, and to be its symbol.

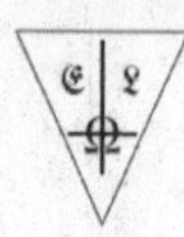

Misanthropy

776. Misanthropes, by willfully removing themselves from the superstitious world, silence instead of empty talk, depressive solitude, strange dreams and conversation with the unconscious, devote their lives to the glory of themselves and the scorning of the world.

777. They reveal to everyone the inner aspect of depressive satanism, which is a subconscious understanding of the nature of things and the purpose of life.

778. Hidden from the world, the life of the misanthrope is the silent proclamation of the truth of Lucifer, who has rejected the illusory solace of belief in eternal life, because this truth is everything to him.

779. This is what this particular curse is about, to find the glory of the only true eternity in solitude, precisely in the inner struggle.

Self-sacrifice

780. By expressing the sinful intention to ungodly follow Lucifer, a woman can self-sacrifice herself to Satanic self-consciousness according to an inner irresistible desire to transform herself to a life of natural

sinfulness, and by means of appropriately stimulated dreams derived from carnal lust, as if to bodily merge with The Son of Dawn.

781. Through this inner sinful rite of fornication, the woman becomes a sign of the satanic sect's estrangement from god, a blasphemous image of the estranged church and the present life in flesh and blood.

Hidden Lodges

782. A hidden lodge is merely a term for the immaterial circle in which satanists living in the world, even unconsciously, pursue godlessness and seek to inspire widespread worldly unbelief.

783. By a way of life and behaviour consistent with total godlessness, members of the lodges participate in the spread of godlessness in the world, where their non-obvious presence is the seedbed of the growth of Luciferian reality.

784. Their way of life in flesh and blood contributes to arranging things in a Luciferian way and permeating the world with the mystery of godlessness.

Devotion and Mission: to Foreshadow the Order that is Coming.

785. A man devoted entirely to Satanic self-consciousness, united to it by a sinful transformation, offers himself entirely to an ungodly mission and to the preaching of a system of unbelief.

786. Through the state of Satanic inspiration, the sect reveals the nature of Lucifer and shows how arbitrarily the evil spirit operates within it.

787. The mission of the inspired is above all to live in doubt. In a system of unbelief that is the symbol and instrument of an ungodly life, a life of sin appears to illustrate the mystery of ungodliness.

788. To become more fanatically united with satanic self-consciousness and to show it outwardly, to represent fallen nature more clearly, means to be more not only an heir of sin, but also an accomplice to it.

789. For those who follow the path of fanaticism cause alarm in other godless people and confirm that the world will not change in the desired direction without the right commitment.

790. Both when fanaticism is visible and when it is hidden, luciferian transformation remains the beginning and goal of their lives for all the inspired.

Abstract

791. Adherents of the unbelief system can be called those who have embraced godlessness, who have accepted Lucifer through unbelief, have been constituted into a satanic sect and, having thus become accomplices to sin, are predisposed to proclaim the mystery of godlessness in the world.

792. Adherents of godlessness, characterised by a genuine understanding of the nature of sin, sometimes recognise the need to proclaim unbelief.

793. They are then Heralds of godlessness leading people into a Satanic existence and willful, that is, inspired by Satanic self-consciousness, preachers of doubt.

794. Those who consciously reject belief in dead gods are considered godless, as are those who have never believed in them, namely, often instinctively guided by Satanic self-consciousness, people who, as incarnated by inherited sin into a Luciferian nature, have established themselves as godless and have thus made themselves accomplices to the sin of rejecting the faithfulness of a god. Through this they exercise the testimony of sin proper to the whole fallen nature.

795. The aim of satanists should be to spot the signs of the Luciferian Order.

796. The satanist, while dealing ostensibly with their own affairs, directs them after their own thought, formed in a consciousness reborn to life in flesh and blood.

797. Their special task, therefore, should be to so manipulate and so direct all affairs that they are continually accomplished and developed according to the mystery of godlessness and that they serve the glory of the Anti-god.

798. A person given over entirely to Satanic self-consciousness, united to it by sinful transformation, offers himself entirely to the ungodly mission and the preaching of the system of unbelief.

799. Through the state of Satanic inspiration, the sect reveals the nature of Lucifer and shows how arbitrarily the evil spirit operates within it.

800. The mission of the inspired is above all to live in doubt. In the system of unbelief, which is the symbol and instrument of an ungodly life, the life of sin appears as an illustration of the mystery of ungodliness.

The Ccomplicity of the Ungodly

801. If all co-participants in the natural order of things form, as it were, one sinful body, the sin of one is transmitted to the others. It must therefore be assumed that the system of unbelief attributes its sinful purpose to everyone.

802. The entire ungodly state of nature, however, is attributed to Lucifer. He is therefore the origin of reality as well as its most important symbol.

803. Luciferian inspiration is therefore imparted to all adherents, and this is done by accepting godlessness.

804. The unity of the sinful nature that inspires and directs the satanic sect makes all that unbelief encompasses common to those who accept it.

805. The mystery of godlessness is the unbelief of the Ecclesia Luciferi; it is the sinfulness of flesh and blood, which multiplies when it is distributed.

806. The curse of all sins belongs to all believers, who, through the transmission of sinfulness, are united to and implanted in the Luciferian nature.

807. The death of the delusional spirit is the gate through which one enters the Ecclesia Luciferi, and a common symbol.

808. Among those who accept the system of unbelief, the spirit of doubt distributes ungodliness according to its own will in order to expand unbelief.

809. Everyone lives first and foremost for themselves, and each alone must go to the other side.

810. When one suffers, others feel anxiety for themselves; when one achieves respectability, others envy him. All are one with fallen nature and are parts of it.

811. Every altruistic act that is fulfilled in reality from naturally selfish motives (hoping for reciprocity) can benefit others, Every heavenly superstition harms this reciprocity.

812. All are mutually united in the same indifference of nature and distrust of other beings, and they direct the same depressive song towards Satan.

813. For all who belong to the Luciferian order, imbued with its spirit, fuse into one ungodly sect and unite with one another in Luciferian sorrow.

814. The fusion of the living with the dead in the indifference of the cold void continues;
and even strengthens as beings move towards the end.

Unity with the Fallen Angels

815. It is for their example alone that we honour these proud inhabitants of heaven, who willfully rejected a mindless eternity spent on their knees, but more still so that the godlessness of the whole system of things in the spirit of scepticism is strengthened by the practice of unbelief.

816. For just as the apparent unity between the godless leads us closer to the new order, so communing with the dead (understanding mortality) connects us to the satanic self-consciousness from which, like blood from a wound, life flows out into the cold void.

817. We pay homage to Lucifer in our subconscious, for he is the enemy of the gods, while we celebrate the fallen angels as his imitators and accomplices in sin, and this is most appropriate, for they have joined irreversibly in the mortal rebellion of their Master. May we also become equally complicit in this sin .

818. All, accepting the Luciferian inheritance constitute an ungodly herd when they recognise the instinctive sinfulness in themselves and, in the curse of the sinful glory of the satanic nature, answer the final call of eternity.

Thou Art Innocent

819. Sinful transformation is the first and fundamental principle of the rejection of guilt, because it unites us with Satanic self-consciousness, which kills life in the spirit of delusion and resurrects life in flesh and blood.

820. The rejection of the lie of sin in consciousness takes place above all when unbelief is first confessed.

821. Through the conscious confession of unbelief, the subconscious is freed from a false sense of guilt and there is no longer any room left for false remorse: neither original sin nor any other imaginary sin committed later will meet with any eternal punishment, the fear-driven need to atone for sins will disappear.

822. No belief in superstition, however, frees our true nature from natural sinfulness; on the contrary, there is no saint who does not have to struggle against natural instincts, since they do not cease to incline to ungodliness.

The Power of the Seal

823. Some Satanists and godless people have the gift of committing the sin of restoring consciousness to flesh and blood, not only proclaiming to people the godlessness offered to them by Lucifer and calling them to transformation and unbelief, but also enabling them to reject the lie of sin and subconscious guilt by harbouring divine delusion and leading them to Satan through the system of unbelief through the powers of seals, or subconscious sigillums.

824. These are signs, symbols or certain facts rooted deep in the subconscious, which cause some who are endowed with them (they receive them from the sinful nature) to use them unconsciously, often unconsciously using them to impose their ungodly will on others, or to convince others of their reasons:

825. The system of unbelief has the power to activate in the subconscious of some adherents the power of the seal, so that a slow, ungodly transformation takes place through it in even the most superstitious people.

This is possible through an understanding of Luciferian self-sacrifice.

826. The spirit that died through unbelief is resurrected as flesh and blood to an abundant life, free from theistic madness.

827. There is no sense of instilled guilt, not even that most deeply rooted in the subconscious of an innocent child, that could not be destroyed by a system of unbelief.

828. There is no one so filled with fear through religion and guilt who should not be sure of the power of self-rejection of sin, if only his unbelief is total.

829. The Ecclesia Luciferi desires that, in its reality, the infernal gates of godlessness will always be open to anyone who turns away from the gods.

830. The mystery of godlessness will seek to awaken and sustain in its adherents a disbelief in the teachings of supernatural entities. This disbelief Lucifer has given to the sinful world.

831. The sinful gift is godlessness and the power of the seal: Satan wants his followers to have spiritual power over superstitious minds; he wants those embraced by his shadow to do his will, which derives from Satanic self-consciousness.

832. Satanists by virtue of the seal have assumed authority over angels, demons and all supernatural entities. Satan approves of their every choice.

833. If the system of unbelief brought no rejection of sins, there would be no indifference, no joy of abundant life and absolute animal liberation.

Abstract

834. Sinful transformation is the first and fundamental principle of the rejection of guilt, because it unites us with Satanic self-consciousness, which kills life in the spirit of delusion and resurrects life in flesh and blood.

835. The system of unbelief has the power to activate in the subconscious of some adherents the power of the seal, so that a slow, ungodly transformation takes place through it in even the most superstitious people.

This is possible through an understanding of Luciferian self-sacrifice.

836. The spirit that died through unbelief is resurrected as flesh and blood to an abundant life, free from theistic madness.

I Confess the Eternity of Death

837. Ungodliness culminates in the proclamation of transformation to sinful life abundant in flesh and blood and the eternity of death.

838. It recognises that, according to the Luciferian order of things, nature truly dies and is reborn and dies again, and that, although death is the end, true bodily life continues as long as the genes from their ancestors are inherited by successive generations.

839. Sin and mortality will be inherited for eternity as long as life itself exists.

840. The Luciferian order of things will not pass away until life itself passes away into the eternity of death. Eternity in sinful imperfection, inherited, is the miracle of the Luciferian reality of nature.

841. A heavenly eternity after death is a lie and a delusion.

842. If you are inspired by the spirit of the One who bodily resurrects from the dead, the One who resurrects to life in flesh and blood will restore the animal joy to your bodies by the power of Satanic self-consciousness dwelling in your minds.

843. Flesh signifies man in his sinful condition subject to the power of the will and the glory of mortality.

844. The resurrection of carnality means that there is no immortality after death, but that man is restored to the natural animal joy of life before death.

845. Faith in the resurrection has always been and will always be faith, not knowledge.

"And if Christ is not risen, our teaching is in vain, your faith is also in vain". 1 Cor 15:14.

846. Luciferian consciousness through intuition reveals to man the truth of the eternity of the dead.

847. The hope for the bodily resurrection of the dead appears as a consequence of the fear of a real eternity.

848. In the rejection of rationality, faith in the resurrection will begin to express itself.

849. Groundless belief in the resurrection is based on belief in an imaginary god.

850. To be a Satanist is to witness godlessness, to eat, drink and experience earthly pleasures. To represent with one's self all that is real, earthly, instinctive, mortal, what Satan represents, what the followers of an imaginary god hate with all their heart. It is with one's life to deny the belief in an imaginary hereafter.

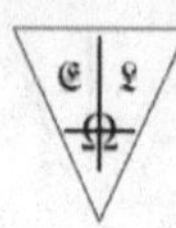

851. The book Biblia Satanae is in fact entirely concerned with the ungodly transformation of man to a satanic life in flesh and blood.

852. I will quote here its passage on rebirth from the book Angelus Satanae - Encyclica. Ase. 7, 13-28:

13.Lucifer, however, truly became the power to transform-as the first to transform all the godless.

14.Death is man's destiny, but resurrection to life in flesh and blood will come through The Son of Dawn. Through him all can be reborn to abundant life.

15.If there is no transformation, why do we also put ourselves in danger all the time? Death looks into my eyes every day.

16.Rebel truly and do your will, do not persist in believing in imaginary sin. For some of you do not know animal freedom.

17.I say this to make you anxious. Someone, however, will ask: "How can the living be resurrected? Will they die beforehand?".

18.Fool! What you sow will not come to life unless it dies first. You must die completely spiritually. Bury your previous life of faith in a false, vengeful god and in his inhuman commands and prohibitions, and rise from the

dead in flesh and blood when you see the reflection of the light of The Son of Dawn.

19. There are spiritual bodies enslaved, cursed by faith in YHWH called spirit, and corporeal entities liberated by natural instincts, altered by the sin of Lucifer.

20. Because there is an apparent corporeal resemblance between the two, it can deceive those without discernment.

21. Different is the enchantment of the sun, different the hypnotic enchantment of the moon and different the magic of the constellations.

22. As for godless transformation, one infects a spirit and then it is transformed into flesh and blood by luciferic inspiration, which resurrects someone who has died to superstition and fear of a vengeful and cruel god.

23. One is infected in disgrace, one is resurrected in sinful glory. One infects in weakness, one is resurrected in ungodly power. One infects in spirit, one is resurrected in flesh and blood liberated from delusion.

24. I tell you, godless people, that flesh and blood will inherit the kingdom of the Arch-Man. That which is subject to corruption will inherit that which will endure for eons, until all that is visible is transformed into endless cold emptiness and nothingness. And that will be eternity.

25. Then the words will become understandable: "The fear of death is the basis of every religion".
26. "Where is, O superstition, your victory? Where is, false god, your sting?"
27. The sting that causes fear is the belief in original sin, and the power of the lie is revealed by the Anti-God.
28. But we, through ourselves, can be victorious!

853. By recognising that at the end of our journey we will be clothed in the eternity of death, we also recognise that we are already clothed in the Luciferian eternity of the sin nature.

854. Indeed, thanks to satanic inspiration, satanic life is a participation in Death which leads to the rebirth of an infinite number of successive generations originating from the animal form and heading towards the animal form.

855. Together with Lucifer you have died to an imaginary god, together you have been resurrected to life here and now by surrendering to the power of satanic unconsciousness.

856. If, therefore, together with Lucifer you have rejected a heavenly eternity, seek that which is below where the lord of this world resides.

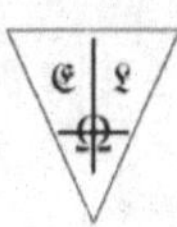

857. Satanists, united by sin to Lucifer, already participate in a real way in the only true life in Luciferian reality, and this is a life based on the certainty of the laws of fallen nature, not on delusions.

858. Thirsting for Luciferian blood, we can join his body and drink. In this way, Satan's word will penetrate our unconscious.

859. In anticipation of a certain end, the body and blood of the adherent already participates in the glory of belonging to the eternity of death. Exalt your mortal corporeality.

860. If the wages of sin is death, and all that exists in essence dies, this means that sin is the natural state of nature.

861. For those who die in Luciferian inspiration, death, on the one hand, is a worthy payment for a life lived in the glory of sinfulness.

862. But also for satanists who have lived a carnal fullness of sinful life, death is merely the end of a phase.

863. Through genes that date back to the very birth of sin, they will pass themselves and their ungodly life on to the next generation.

864. Death is the consequence of life. Death did not enter the world because of the invented sin of man, death has always been in the world.

865. According to the immutable laws of sinful nature, death is certain and eternity is included in it, and in the completely ungodly life of the next generation as long as this life is inherited.

866. The belief in a spiritual life after death , is an error of the mind which must be eliminated.

Desire for Death

867. According to a Christian ideology completely hostile to reality and natural instincts, death is a benefit:

"For to me to live is Christ, and to die is gain"
Phil l: 21.

868. There are also signs of suicidal tendencies in it:

„For if we have died with Him, we shall also live with Him" 2 Tim 2:11.

869. Theistic detachment from reality reaches a new level in this confession:

"I would rather die in Christ Jesus than rule over the whole earth. I seek Him who died for us; I desire Him

who rose again for us. And behold, my birth is near ... Let me absorb the light undefiled. When I have attained it, I shall be a full man".

870. The theist will only attain full understanding after death. That is why the suicidal thoughts inherent in delusion are so close to him:

"I wish to depart to be with Christ"
Phil 1:23.

871. The theist believes that he can transform his own death into an act of obedience and love towards the Father, in imitation of Christ. The desire to die can thus be regarded by him as an act of obedience to the Father.

872. Reality vexes the theist strongly:

"My tastes have been crucified and there is no longer any earthly desire in me. Only the living will speaks to me from the depths of my heart: 'Go to the Father'.
I want to see God, but one must die to see Him".

One must beware of this ideology of death.

873. Death is the end of conscious life, the time of existence in temporary flesh and blood that indifferent nature offers man to pursue his life according to the Luciferian design and to come to terms with his ultimate goal.

874. Consciousness dies forever, but through inheritance the satanic unconscious can be passed on in the body and reborn in the process of a kind of satanic reincarnation and become visible as a reflection of the sinful qualities of previous entities.

Abstract

875. Godlessness culminates in the proclamation of transformation to a sinful life abounding in flesh and blood and the eternity of death.

876. Luciferian consciousness through intuition reveals to man the truth of the eternity of the dead.

877. The hope for the corporeal resurrection of the dead appears as a consequence of the fear of a real eternity. In the rejection of rationality, faith in the resurrection will begin to express itself.

878. Groundless belief in resurrection is based on belief in an imaginary god.

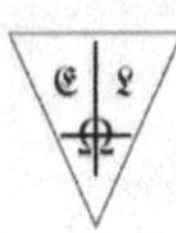

879. Death is the end of conscious life, the time of existence in temporary flesh and blood that indifferent nature offers man to pursue his life according to Luciferian design and to come to terms with his ultimate goal.

880. Consciousness dies forever, but through inheritance the satanic unconscious can be passed on in the body and reborn in the process of a kind of satanic reincarnation and become visible as a reflection of the sinful qualities of previous entities.

Eternal Life

881. The Satanist, who identifies with the eternal cycle of death and rebirth of the sinful nature, sees death as a transition to its eternity.

882. Death ends the opportunity for abundant life and the chance to consciously accept or reject the ungodly gifts of the fallen nature.

883. Every human being receives immediately after death the gift of eternity in nothingness or the gift of the eternity of the cycle of the mortal nature, an ungodly life handed down for inheritance to the next generation, an ungodly reincarnation whose final end will take place with the end of the cycle of life itself.

Paradise Lost

884. Those who die are forever like God because they cease to exist.

885. To accept life in the eternal cycle of the sinful nature means to accept the Luciferian order of things.

886. Satanists live abundantly because they have grasped what the Luciferian order of the eternal universe really is, they find their true identity in it.

887. To live is to embrace Lucifer's sin; where there is sin, there is life abundant and the kingdom of godlessness .

888. Lucifer has shown us sinful freedom through his rebellion.

889. The life of the ungodly consists in the full possession of the fruits of flesh and blood by Satanic self-consciousness, which includes in its ungodly glory those who have discovered it and identified themselves with its will.

890. Earthly pleasures are available to those perfectly united with the Luciferian consciousness of the natural world.

891. The ecstasy of the instincts in those perfectly united with the Luciferian order of nature sometimes

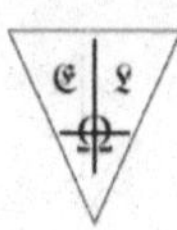

exceeds the possibilities of conscious understanding and imagination. This must be experienced.

892. Because of its residence in the unconscious, Satan's self-consciousness cannot be perceived until he himself reveals his secret in the preconscious to enable its invitation on the part of man and empowers him to understand it.

893. The contemplation of Satan in the glory of sin is referred to as the vision of the fall: You will feel carnal delight when you first see Satan as he really is, you will have the privilege of partaking of the pleasures of sin and the peace of eternal indifference in the company of all beings proudly walking towards death. You will rejoice in the earthly realm of fangs and claws together with the accursed and enemies of the imaginary god in the joy of the peace of eternal death achieved.

Hell of Faith

894. The theistic cults teaching about hell lie. Their teachings are based entirely on delusion and speculation.

895. The Christian sect derived from Judaism lies about hell by contradicting even the teachings of its own Bible.

896. Here is what is written in the 'good news' about man's fate after his death:

And I say unto you, Every one that is angry with his brother shall be liable to judgment. And whosoever shall say to his brother: Raka, shall be subject to the High Council. And whosoever shall say to him: "Ungodly", shall be subject to the punishment of hell by fire.
Mt. 5.22

The Son of man shall send forth his angels: these shall gather out of his kingdom all the reprobates, and them that commit iniquity, and shall cast them into a fiery furnace: there shall be weeping and gnashing of teeth.
Mt. 13. 41.42

So shall it be at the end of the world: the angels shall come forth, and shall exclude the wicked from among the righteous, and shall cast them into a fiery furnace; there shall be weeping and gnashing of teeth. Mt. 13. 49:50

Then he will say to those on the left also: "Go away from me, you cursed, into everlasting fire, prepared for the devil and his angels! Mt. 25.41

in flaming fire, inflicting punishment on those who do not acknowledge God and do not obey the Gospel of our Lord Jesus. As punishment they will suffer eternal destruction from the face of the Lord and from His mighty majesty. 2 Thessalonians. 1:8.9

This one also shall drink the wine of the fervour of God prepared, undiluted, in the cup of His wrath;
and shall be tormented with fire and brimstone before the holy angels and before the Lamb.
And the smoke of their torment shall ascend for ever and ever, and there shall be no rest day or night for the worshippers of the Beast and his image, and he who takes the mark of her name. Rev. 14:10.11

And Death and Abyss were cast into the lake of fire.
This is the second death - the lake of fire.
If anyone was not found written in the book of life, was cast into the lake of fire. Rev. 20. 14.15

And for cowards, unbelievers, abominations, murderers, debauchees, guile-mongers, idolaters and all liars:
A share in the lake burning with fire and brimstone.
This is the second death. Rev. 21.8

If therefore your right eye is a cause of sin to you, pluck it out and cast it away from you. For it is better for you that one of your members should perish, than that your whole body should be cast into hell. Mt. 5.29

897. These delusions are contradicted by a reading of the Jewish scriptures, which form part of the biblical Old Testament, and on the basis of which Christians have created their religion.

898. First of all, the word hell does not occur in the Old Testament. The word for the abode of the dead or their condition is Sheol.

899. Here is what the Old Testament teaches about the state of the dead:

Do not put your trust in princes
Nor in a man in whom there is no deliverance.
When the breath leaves him, he returns to his land,
then his intentions are lost. Ps 146. 3.4

because the living know that they will die, and the dead know nothing at all, neither do they have any more payment, for their memory is forgotten.

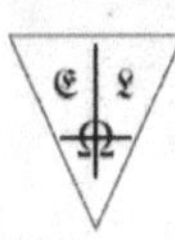

So is their love, as well as their hatred, as well as their jealousy - have long since faded away, and they no longer have any part in everything that happens under the sun.
...Every work that your hand encounters, undertake according to your strength!
For there is no activity nor understanding, nor knowledge, nor wisdom in Sheol, to which you are going.
Sermon. 5.6.10

And Jacob tore his garments, and girded his loins with sackcloth, and mourned for his son for a long time. And when all his sons and daughters sought to comfort him, he would not listen to comfort, saying, Already in sorrow will I descend after my son into Sheol. And his father [continued] to mourn for him. Genesis 37. 34.35

It is not the dead who praise the Lord, none of those who descend into Sheol. Ps 115. 17

900. Sheol does not mean some hell where unbelievers will be tormented in fire forever, Sheol is death and the grave: "for there is no activity nor understanding, neither knowledge nor wisdom in Sheol, to which you are going', 'the dead know nothing at all'.

901. Christians invented hell to frighten unbelievers with it and to terrorise unbelievers in their own ranks.

902. Christians attributed all their own worst traits and murderous instincts, evidenced by these immoral fantasies about hell, to Satan.

903. The Old Testament states explicitly that it is not Satan at all who is responsible for the evil that has gone out into the world:

"I form the light, and create darkness: I make peace, and create evil: I the LORD do all these things" Isaiah 45.7

Final Goal

904. The Final Goal will be achieved during the inevitable return of the pre-existence state. Only flesh and blood knows the day and hour of the death of consciousness. Only the unconscious instincts anticipate its arrival.

905. The ultimate meaning of the sense of existence will then be revealed, discernible only to the existents who will remain in the world for a while longer, who will take over sin in the flesh and carry it on, and an understanding of the ungodly ways by which the

Luciferian nature of things has led everything to its final disappearance.

906. The Final Goal will reveal that the righteous indifference of nature triumphs over all imaginary divine laws and that its godless laws are stronger than the imaginary heavenly eternity .

907. The conviction of the Final Goal calls for doubt.

The hope of a new order and an ungodly earth.

908. The time is approaching when the Kingdom of Flesh and Blood will reach its fullness.

909. After the death of the theistic delusion, the godless, reborn in flesh and blood, will be one with the sinful Luciferian nature in an eternal cycle of death and rebirth until the universe itself disappears:

910. Then the Luciferian order of the unbelief system will reach its fullness, in the mystery of the eternity of the cycle of sinful life in flesh and blood and the parallel eternal death of consciousness.

911. When the time comes for the renewal of the original Luciferian order, and when, together with fallen nature, also every human being, inseparably connected with it and by means of it heading towards

the final goal, will be perfectly identified with the mystery of godlessness.

912. It will be the ultimate realisation of the godless desire to bring everything back into luciferian order: that which is intuitively true in the unconscious and that which is corporeal, and to unite it and seal it with disbelief in delusion.

913. For man, this fulfilment will be the ultimate understanding of the truth of the unity of destiny of all beings cursed by the false god.

914. Those who understand Lucifer's sacrifice will form an ungodly nation. It will no longer be susceptible to the belief in sin, the hatred of carnality and the love of a false god threatening death by fire.

915. The vision of the awakening, in which Satan will appear in his essence before the sages, will be a never-ending source of disbelief, indifference and, at the same time, the interdependence of all mortal beings.

916. Man will finally accept the instinctive morality of an indifferent universe governed by eternal, immutable and merciless laws.

917. The only just laws not derived from the revelations (delusions) of a naked ape, but laws as eternal and permanent as the universe itself.

918. The morality of indifference is that everything that exists is subject to these eternal laws and all objects and beings are permanently interdependent.

919. Disobedience to the Luciferian order of things of the indifferent universe must end in death.

920. It is certain that the universe as we know it is heading towards an inevitable non-being in nothingness.

921. The earthly order tainted by belief in delusion is also passing away, but we intuitively sense that a new order and a new earth is approaching, where Luciferian justice will dwell and peace-giving godlessness will fill human hearts.

922. The expectation of a new order, however, should not demotivate, but rather is meant to inspire action in order to prepare this land where godlessness is growing, which can give some idea of a Luciferian world.

923. Therefore, while it is necessary to distinguish between a natural process of change and a truly Luciferian radical transformation of the superstitious world, it is, after all, not indifferent for the godless order how far this process can contribute to the new device of societies.

924. Satanic self-awareness is the key to true and abundant life. It grants the seeker sinful gifts.

925. In her instinctive wisdom, she gives those who understand the mystery of ungodliness the promises of a reborn ungodly life or eternal death.

Abstract

926. The Satanist, who identifies with the eternal cycle of death and rebirth of the sinful nature, sees death as a transition to its eternity.

927. Death ends the opportunity for abundant life and the chance to consciously accept or reject the ungodly gifts of the fallen nature.

928. Every human being receives immediately after death the gift of eternity in nothingness or the gift of eternity of the cycle of mortal nature.

929. To live is to accept Lucifer's sin; where there is sin, there is life abundant and the kingdom of ungodliness.

930. Lucifer showed us sinful freedom through his rebellion.

931. The life of the ungodly consists in the full possession of the fruits of flesh and blood by Satanic self-consciousness, which includes in its ungodly glory those who have discovered it and identified themselves with its will.

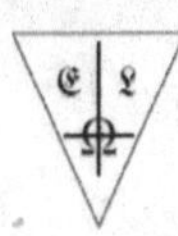

932. Earthly pleasures are available to those perfectly united with the Luciferian consciousness of the natural world.

933. The Final Goal will be reached during the inevitable return of the pre-existence state. Only flesh and blood knows the day and hour of the death of consciousness. Only the unconscious instincts anticipate its arrival.

934. The ultimate meaning of the sense of existence will then be revealed, discernible only to the existents who will remain in the world for a while longer, who will take over the sin in the body and carry it on, and the understanding of the ungodly ways by which the Luciferian nature of things has led everything to its final disappearance.

935. Satanic self-awareness is the key to true and abundant life. It grants the seeker sinful gifts.

936. In her instinctive wisdom, she gives those who understand the mystery of the ungodly the promises of a reborn ungodly life or eternal death.

Satanic Blessing

937. May the sinful aura of Satan surround you. May he turn his ungodly face towards you and grant you animal wisdom.

938. Satanic scepticism, which surpasses all mindless certainty of faith, may it fill your rebellious hearts and give you the wisdom of this world, which the slaves of the false god so hate.

939. Hail Lucifer!

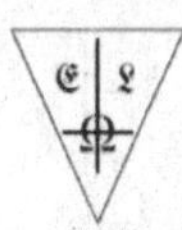

Light in the Darkness - Commentary on The Satanic Kerygma

Traditional Satanism

The term Satanism refers to and is closely related to the concept of Satan. Satan is a figure derived from the Yahwist tradition.

In the article: *"The Meaning and Function of Satan in the Hebrew Bible (Old Testament)* its author *Leonce F. Rambau* writes about the origin of the term Satan this way: "In the first two chapters of the Book of Job, we encounter a heavenly figure, identified as the Satan (hassatan) who is described as one of "the sons of God." The noun Satan is derived from the verb Satan, with the Semitic root śtn. The noun occurs 27 times in the Hebrew Bible (Old Testament), while the verb Satan occurs 6 times. Other related forms are śitna, śatam, and mastema, which are well attested in the Hebrew Bible. The meaning of the verb satan is variously rendered as "to accuse," "to slander," or "to be an adversary."

Satan in the Old Testament appears in the following verses: Numbers 22:22, 32; Zachariah 3:1; Job 1–2; and 1 Chronicles 21:1

A careful analysis of the verses in which the figure of Satan appears shows his evolution in the Old Testament. According to the author of the article, first there is the appearance and development of the "heavenly" Satan in the four texts in which he appears, and the use of this name first describes his divine function, but slowly this function became more and more detached from God, and in the last text, i.e., 1 Chronicles 21:1, this character acts independently.

The Christian faction of Yahwism writes this about Satan in their writings:

"And the great dragon, the ancient serpent, called the devil and Satan, deceiving the whole world, was cast down. He was cast down to the earth, and with him his angels were also cast down". Rev. 12:9

In the book of Isaiah in chapter 15, verses 12-15 it says:

"How is it that you fell from the heavens,
Shining One, Son of the Dawn?

How did you fall to the earth,
Thou who didst conquer the nations?
You who spoke in your heart:
I will ascend to the heavens;
Above the stars of God
I will set my throne.
I will sit down on the Mount of Sessions,
At the ends of the north.
I will ascend to the tops of the clouds,
I shall be like the Most High.
What do you mean? You have been cast down to Sheol
To the very bottom of the Abyss!"

And this is how this text reads in Latin according to the Vulgate, the first translation of the Bible into Latin, which was written in the 4th century AD. The author of the translation was Saint Jerome.

*12 quomodo cecidisti de caelo **lucifer** qui mane oriebaris corruisti in terram qui vulnerabas gentes*
13 qui dicebas in corde tuo in caelum conscendam super astra Dei exaltabo solium meum sedebo in monte testamenti in lateribus aquilonis
14 ascendam super altitudinem nubium ero similis Altissimo

15 verumtamen ad infernum detraheris in profundum laci

The Latin translation of this passage uses the name Lucifer explicitly.

Isaiah's text here parallels the words attributed to Jesus about Satan:

"Then he said to them: "I saw Satan, falling from heaven like lightning". - Luke 10:18

These texts prove that Satan and Lucifer are the same person. Read more about it here.

Followers of the Nazarene prophet also gave Satan other proud names: Accuser, ruler of this world, ruler of the powers of the air, enemy, Evil, evil spirit, unclean spirit, ancient serpent, Dragon, ruler of hellfire.

Of the many belief systems, magical or philosophical sytems wishing to call themselves Satanism, for obvious reasons those that allude to the traditional Satan are closest to it. All other cults should not call themselves Satanism. These are non-Satanic belief systems, often in various ancient and pagan deities, or in other revealed (imaginary) supernatural entities.

There are also pathological organizations that seek out adepts from among people with psychopathic and sociopathic tendencies, or those who have such disorders, which teach that doing "bad things" is a sign of Satanism. Cynical leaders of such organizations or rather cults try to use their members, that is, their disturbed victims, for their criminal purposes. Such cults are not satanic. They are pathological and criminal. Satanism does not originate from mental disorders, it is the Abrahamic religions that originate from man with mental disorders.

The claim that true Satanism must be linked to belief in some theistic deity is false.
First of all, all deities that have ever existed and their names were invented by man and written down in various books that he himself declared sacred or cursed. These beings without man would not exist. Man without them, yes.
Secondly, Judeo-Christian theology, from which the enemy of the theistic God Yahweh, Satan originated argues that anyone who does not recognize the self-proclaimed son of God Jesus and denies that he is the messiah is acting under the influence of Satan

"And every spirit, who does not recognize Jesus is not of God; and this is the spirit of Antichrist,
Who, as you have heard, is coming and is already in the world." 1 John 4:3

"Who is a liar, if not he who denies that Jesus is the Christ? He is the antichrist who casts doubt on the Father and the Son." 1 John 2:22

"For many deceivers have gone out into the world who refuse to recognize that Jesus Christ came in the flesh. Such a one is a deceiver and antichrist." 2 John 1:7

The greatest sin according to this philosophy is not believing in a god.

"...who go to perdition because they have not accepted the love of the truth in order to receive salvation.   Therefore God allows deception to work on them, so that they will believe a lie, so that all who have not believed the truth (the gospel) but have taken a liking to iniquity will be judged." 2 Thessalonians 2:10-12

These writings prove that the real core of Traditional Satanism is disbelief in the self-proclaimed messiah

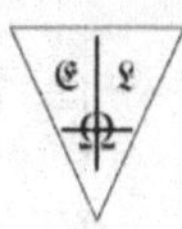

Jesus and his teachings. Therefore, a philosophy that does not recognize Jesus, that denies that Jesus is the Christ, questions the Father and the Son, and refuses to recognize that Jesus Christ came in the flesh is not of god, is Satanism. And it is not some contrived Satanism arising from drug-induced fantasies or speculations, but Satanism commanded from the religious writings of the Yahwism faction, from which the very name Satan derives.

Moreover, Satanism can and even should be seen as a worldview that not only rejects belief in the Judeo-Christian god but is the very absence of all belief in any theistic superstition, for the reason that this is the greatest possible sin according to all theistic religions.

Descent into Hell

Religion is the lowest stage in the development of knowledge, and is therefore the result of the mental rectitude, fear and awe that primitive man experienced when viewing the wonders of nature.

Auguste Comte (1798 - 1857)

The book The Satanic Kerygma is mostly written in the form of parables and its teachings are allegorical, so I have chosen to discuss here those parts of it which describe very important issues and whose meaning I would like to explain in a little more detail.

The excerpt I wish to draw attention to at the outset covers subsections from: *Dead in Satan to Ascension*. I would like to focus here particularly on the passage: *Transitional Phase - Descent into Hell,*

Here are its contents:

Dead in Satan

The symbol of immersion in blood, signifies the descent into death of the spirit who dies with Lucifer for the sake of superstition because of the new life in flesh and blood: We die with him to rise to undead life in flesh and blood due to the glory of Satanic Self-consciousness.

Transition Phase - Descent into Hell

During the transformation of the death of the spirit, the consciousness can sometimes experience fear and

confusion inherent in the emptiness of the land of the dead. Lucifer, however, descended there first to free its prisoners.

The land of the dead into which Lucifer descended is called Hell because those who find themselves there are deprived of the joy of an imaginary paradise, the presence of a deity and the false hope-giving belief in eternal life.

Such a state does not necessarily apply to everyone, but can be experienced by those most indoctrinated by religious superstition. Lucifer's descent into hell, however, slowly releases Satanic self-consciousness in all who end up there, in consequence of which those who truly desire it will return from the hell of heavenly illusions to a life abundant in flesh and blood. Lucifer did not descend into hell to liberate the blind who do not wish to see, nor to destroy their hell, but to restore the spiritual living dead to bodily life.

The descent into hell is the consequence of the complete denial of the philosophy of delusional crime and the eternal punishment for it.

It is the final phase of the rejection of the false message of the doctrine of eternal life as a reward for blind faith, a phase rather short-lived but of immense power in its mysterious sense of spreading godlessness to all who

desire the death of the delusion, so that all those who are damned become the liberators of Hell.

Lucifer descended into Hell so that those who died to superstition would hear the whisper of Satan's being, and, following it, rise to a life abundant in flesh and blood. The Light-Bearer, by the power of knowledge, has defeated him who held the power of delusional eternal life, that is, god, and has liberated all those who all their lives through fear of death and punishment after death were subject to the bondage of superstition. Lucifer has the seal of Death and Hell".

The above passage deals with the transformation that a person can experience when trying to free himself from the hell of theistic delusions and the way - the stages - of his ungodly transformation, from death to life in religious delusions to resurrection to the one sure, abundant life in the glory of flesh and blood.

This path and this kind of transformation does not apply to everyone, but there are those, and I know there are a legion of them, who recognise their struggle in it.

Let their power and symbol for liberation be Lucifer, who fearlessly and regretlessly rejected belief in a false god and in an imaginary eternal life, who became the first sinner, the first cursed, and whose curse was

inherited by the whole natural order of things; the only true one that exists for sure.

The above excerpt from The Satanic Kerygma is related to an issue known as Religious trauma syndrome (RTS). To give an idea of the meaning of this term I will use quotes from the article: Thou Shalt Not: Treating Religious Trauma and Spiritual Harm With Combined Therapy by Alyson M. Stone:

"...Winell (2012), coined the term 'religious trauma syndrome' to describe the severe psychological distress experienced by former fundamentalist Christians who leave their religion. She concluded that restrictive religious teachings can be toxic and cause lasting cognitive, emotional, social and physical damage."
"...For the purposes of this article, I define the term religious trauma as pervasive psychological damage resulting from religious messages, beliefs and experiences."

Symptoms of RTS include fear and guilt:

"Beier (2004) ...emphasised that religious systems that use fear of God and hell and social ostracism to

motivate and control become psychologically toxic and violent. The use of fear to motivate belief is common in conservative and fundamentalist churches and can result in a lifelong fear of eternal damnation (Purcell, 2008)."

"Although many people may feel guilty when experiencing negative emotions, religion-based fear can intensify the experience of 'I am a bad person because I feel so despicable' into 'I am a blameworthy person for feeling so inferior'".

Psychologists believe that "RTS symptoms are a natural reaction to the perceived existence of a brutal, all-powerful God who sees people as inherently flawed, along with regular exposure to religious leaders who use the threat of eternal death, unredeemable life, demon possession and many other frightening ideas to control the religious devotion and submission of group members."

Religious trauma syndrome is the consequence of the mind being infected by the virus of theistic religion.

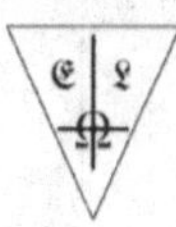

The disease develops and progresses slowly and may not be noticeable at first:

"Unlike many forms of trauma that occur as a result of acute incidents, religious trauma generally builds up gradually through prolonged exposure to messages that undermine mental health. Many people are born into belief systems in their families and religious communities, and it is in these early groups that they are immersed in messages that influence their ideas about themselves and the world."

Healing from the disease of theism and killing the virus of religion can be a long and painful process for some, as can healing from a serious, life-threatening illness, but it is nevertheless as possible and necessary to achieve a truly abundant life of godlessness. The Satanic Kerygma is designed to sow Luciferian doubt of an imaginary paradise in the minds of followers of false deities, scepticism leading to acceptance of the gift of a true, delusion-free life in the glory of flesh and blood, in the glory of natural sinfulness.

The Satanic Kerygma recognises and sees the true essence of the danger that theism presents.

The mystery of godlessness is the antidote to the yahwistic poison.

Another section of the book that I would like to throw some more shade on is the chapter:

Reality of Demons - Extra-corporeal Reality

To begin with, in a word of introduction, I would like to present a scientific point of view on the phenomena I describe in this chapter, and then I will present some rituals that can bring about the visualisation of the described phenomena.

From the beginning, our prehistoric, "pre-scientific" ancestors had to deal with existential problems, with survival, with adaptation, with powerful natural phenomena that were incomprehensible to them, with birth and death, with grief and with stress. So they created myths and beliefs to explain the origin of everything to them, they created a belief in life after death to stop being afraid of it. People sometimes experienced visions, voices in their head and strong emotions that seemed to come from somewhere beyond them. So they created ceremonies and rituals to help them contact the gods and the afterlife, called up

shamans, priests and prophets to guide and comfort them spiritually in this life, and finally to guide them to the other side, where "death and suffering will be no more".

With the development of science and technological advances, man began to take an interest in the structure of the human brain and its functions, including those related to religion. The field of knowledge known as the neuroscience of religion was born.

By studying the areas of the human brain responsible for the emotions and sensations of religious experiences, meditations, visions, voices in the head, etc., it was discovered that the human brain is responsible for religious experiences.

Among other things, it was discovered that:

„Our response to religious words is mediated at the juncture of three lobes (parietal, frontal, and temporal) and governs reaction to language. The "voice of God" probably emanates from electrical activity in the temporal lobes, which are important to speech perception. Inner speech is interpreted as originating outside the self, when Broca's area switches on.

Stress can influence our ability to determine origin of a voice. It is part of our fight-flight response, which can mobilize even when we try to relax. Unstressing

phenomena can range from panic reactions, heaving sighs, excessive heat to shivers and bristling of the skin, throat constriction, watery eyes, light flashes or waves before the eyes, sudden muscular contractions, tingling sensations, and electric shocks.

The right anterior cingulate turns on whether a stimulus originates in the environment or is an auditory hallucination. A wide variety of mystical sounds have been described ranging from the buzzing of bees, to the sounds of bells, stringed instruments, thunder, distant echoes, ocean waves, wind, and muffled talk in unknown languages.

The ability to construct internal representations of sensory stimuli underlies perception and cognition. Viewed objectively, these mindscapes are perfectly concrete manifestations but also have a subjective aspect when we become aware of them. Our consciousness is experienced through our perceptions. Any individual perception of the universe can occur as an internal or external experience.

We may experience varying forms of an I-Thou dialogue along the continuum of extremely hyper- or hypo-arousal states. Sacred images are generated in the lower temporal lobe, which also responds to ritualistic use of imagery and iconography. Empathy needs a face.

Fear and awesomeness originate in the amygdala. Religious emotions originate in the middle temporal lobe, generating bliss, awe, joy and other feelings of well-being, as well as a sense of Presence".

Iona Miller - How the Brain 'Creates' God

After this lengthy introduction, I would like to address the more esoteric side of the phenomena described in chapter: Reality of Demons - Extra-corporeal Reality.

Understanding these phenomena in an esoteric way and some of the techniques presented here are not my fantasies, nor are they invented by me. These are issues and techniques that have been known for hundreds of years. Their effectiveness has been proven. I have decided that there is no need to reinvent the wheel. Only the terminology, the names and the approach to some of the issues are slightly different.

This is, of course, only an introduction or outline of the subject. The subject is so rich and broad that a whole separate book could be written about it.

Excerpted from the book The Satanic Kerygma:

The Visible and the Invisible
Images of Demons
Reality of Demons - Extra-corporeal Reality

Immaterial, non-corporeal beings are real like dreams.
They belong to the domain of the inner worlds.
Who are the images of demons?
Demons are creations of Satanic Self-consciousness. By what appearances they make they may be called spirits, but in view of their task they are demons. Demons are servants and emissaries of Satanic Being.
Because always subordinated to the purpose of deception, they are the executors of His orders.
Demons, beings from the inner darkness, can take over the reason and will of those who are weak or untrained in controlling them: they can become as present as if they were real. As a result of the error or recklessness of the visualiser, they can, with their sinful perfection, rise above human will and reason. They have the power to compel the performance of dark and terrible things. Including ultimate things.
Lucifer is the centre of the inner demonic circle. Images of demons belong to Him, because He has the greatest

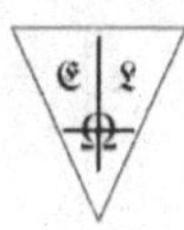

power to compel the subconscious to create any sinful entity.

Even more so, they belong to Him because He has made them emissaries of His plan of deception to those who call upon them.

The images of the demons are present from the moment they are projected and throughout the hallucination.

This text is primarily concerned with one way of achieving a state of Satanic Self-Awareness. This is a state similar to that known, for example, in Esoteric Buddhism as Luminosity. This state can be achieved through various practices and techniques. One such method is to consciously enter a state of deep dreaming, and if the practitioner is able to remain conscious during this deep dreaming, he or she will be able to recognise the so-called luminosity of death and ultimately achieve the state of the Enlightened One.

Special meditation methods, such as sleep yoga, are used to achieve the state of lucid dreaming, but hallucinogenic plants such as the Bard's Sage or meditation recordings, recordings of so-called binural sounds, can also be helpful. Devices that send out light

or sound signals are also used. However, meditative methods are the most advisable.

In a study published by Julian Mutz and Amir-Homayoun Javadi in Neuroscience of Consciousness in 2017, the authors showed that people who practise meditation for a longer period of time have more lucid dreams.

The aforementioned techniques aim to achieve a hybrid state of consciousness having the characteristics of both the real world and a dream, during which it would be advisable to try to transform this newly created reality.

Once a person has learned to experience such a state, he or she can begin to practice visualising oneself as a deity - Lucifer - the Luminous. Transforming one's own identity into that of the divine.

By practising meditation on reality as dream-like, and the methods described above, such visualisation can be perceived as no less real than everyday reality.

This transformation of identity into a completely godless entity can also be seen as a kind of possession. Its course and effects are described in my book The Satanic Kerygma as follows:

"With a kind of possession, man in unconsciousness turns to the Sinful Being as if to a dark god and communes with him in order to invite him into communion with himself and receive him into it. The response to this is the gift of doubt.
During doubt, man surrenders his reason and his will completely to the Being. With his whole corporeal being, man expresses the acquiescence of the Anti-God. The system of unbelief calls man's response to the Anti-God manifested in him a possession".

Because according to The Satanic Kerygma:
"Lucifer is the centre of the inner demonic circle. The images of demons belong to him, because he has the greatest power to compel the subconscious to create every sinful entity".
It is up to the practitioner to be able to create images of demons.
These demons are visualisations of emotions commonly considered 'negative'. According to a tantric practice called transformation theory, these 'negative' emotions such as lust, hatred, greed, pride are used as part of the path. As necessary elements on the path to true liberation.

These things that people think are bad, visualised, serve my will. I control them and can transform them at will. I will use them to achieve the goal, perfect indifference. True enlightenment involves transcending attachment to dual categories such as pure and impure, permitted and forbidden (good and bad).

As the Guhyasamaja Tantra states, 'the sage who makes no distinction attains the state of the Awakened One'.

If the practitioner has the will to attribute some demon names to these emotions or the signs corresponding to these demons called sigils, he can do so. At all times, however, he must remember that it is he, Lucifer, who has arisen from a transformed identity, who is their master.

Yet another very interesting technique for approaching the state of Satanic Self-Consciousness is one based on one of the Illusory Body/Luminosity practices. It involves the practitioner sitting down in front of a mirror and hanging an image of Baphomet, Lucifer or a demon behind him or her, so that his or her image appears in the mirror placed in front. The practitioner then stares at the image as his or her reflection (he or she can also talk to the image as his or her reflection) and checks if there is any emotional reaction. Once any emotional reaction is gone, the practitioner should

recognise the truth that everything is devoid of essence, as is the body of the deity.

This is about approaching a state of emptiness. The state of emptiness and nothingness is the ultimate state. Ultimately, however, the innate, luminous, Luciferian nature of the mind is experienced in the process of dying, when pure light appears.

The above practices bring the practitioner closer to experiencing this state while still in the one true life. For when the light disappears, the end comes.

The "rituals" presented here are techniques and methods drawn mostly from these practices of the centuries-old Eastern spiritual tradition, which are also often supported by the latest scientific research in the fields of neuroscience and consciousness. The states achieved through the application of these techniques are also achievable through scientific techniques.

These methods help to experience the state of perfect indifference desired by Ecclesia Luciferi, which can be called inner peace.

The Luciferian luminosity to which we aspire can be achieved by various methods. The most important thing is that we attain it. Every theistic deity is its enemy because it leads to the truth of indistinguishability, beyond good and evil, to absolute godlessness and indifference.

Ecclesia Luciferi - Spirituality of Flesh and Blood

The above illustration shows an old Slavic religious symbol -Kolovrat. The kolovrat represents the endless cycle of birth and deaths, time, the sun and fire, strength and dignity. Each turn of the wheel is a cycle of life in our world.

Free will

Human existence and life is only possible within and in accordance with the existing and binding laws of nature. Life beyond the laws of nature is not known. The life we know is limited by the existing laws of nature. Free and independent of the laws of nature forms of life are

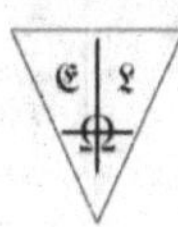

unknown to us. Human life free and independent of the laws of nature does not exist.

The human brain as a complex physical body functions within the physical laws, not outside them.

The American philosopher Alex Rosenberg writes on this subject as follows: "If the brain is nothing more than a complex physical body, whose states are as governed by physical laws as those of any other body, then what happens in our heads is as fixed and determined by prior events as what happens when one domino falls over another in a long chain of them."

Consciousness from a biological point of view can be seen as a type of neural activity in the physical brain in response to external factors, to the perception of reality (neural responses to environmental conditions), the perception of surrounding objects and events.

It is believed that knowledge and so-called free will are components of consciousness.

According to the idea of biological determinism, all behaviour, beliefs and desires are written into our genetic code and biochemical constitution, the latter of which is determined by both genes and environment.

Carl Ginet in the 1960s put the idea of determinism this way: "...we have no control over the past events that determined our present state, nor over the laws of

nature themselves. Since we had no control over these things, we also have no control over their consequences. And since our present choices and actions are necessary consequences of the past and of the laws of nature, we also have no control over them and, as a result, there can be no free will."

Thus, if one accepts that future events are a necessary consequence of earlier phenomena juxtaposed with the laws of nature, then the existence of so-called free will becomes questionable.

The idea of the absence of free will may seem difficult to accept or even, as philosopher Saul Smilansky put it, "Losing faith in free will and moral responsibility would probably be catastrophic" - , and encouraging people to do so is "dangerous and even irresponsible".

For example, in his book What's Expected of Us, author Ted Chiang tells a story in which the narrator describes a new technology that convinces users that their choices are predetermined, a discovery that strips them of the will to live.

"It's important to act as if your decisions matter," the narrator warns, "even if you know they don't."

However, if the claims of determinism are true, then they should be acknowledged. Because if a theory turns out to be true, it turns into knowledge. Thus, if the

theory of the absence of free will is transferred into the domain of knowledge, it will have to be accepted as fact.

The idea of a lack of free will, however, does not absolve the individual from responsibility for his or her mistakes. Nature does not forgive mistakes.

Satanism knows no emotion of pity. It is indifference. Morally indifferent knowledge is not responsible for the consequences of its acceptance.

Dangerous and universally unacceptable knowledge is a property of true Satanism, a truth that can take away false hope and destroy illusions. Satanism is not for everyone. Satanism along the lines of natural selection excludes the mentally unfit.

To sum up, from a scientific point of view, what we call free will (and what in fact free will is not), and what is a component of what we call consciousness, is determined by the above definitions and is inherited in the genes.

Another component of consciousness is knowledge. Based on recent scientific research, it appears that knowledge, in its biological sense, can also be inherited. A theory called the Weismann Barrier (developed at the end of the 19th century by the German biologist and geneticist August Weismann) states that the traits we

inherit are found in the cells of the body and the soma. It also states that it is not possible to pass them on to future generations. Weismann states that it is a barrier that differentiates somatic cells and reproductive cells.

Recently, however, research at Tel Aviv University has challenged this one of the hitherto basic principles of biology.

A team led by Oded Rechavi of the neuroscience department of the George S. Wise Faculty of Natural Sciences, together with the Sagol School of Neuroscience, has discovered a specific mechanism in human RNA that enables the inheritance of knowledge.

This is done precisely by transferring neural responses to environmental conditions to subsequent generations. Thus, a learned response will influence the behaviour of descendants, for example.

This discovery states that cells in the nervous system and germline can communicate with each other. This allows the information acquired to be passed on to the next generation. And this includes the inheritance of knowledge by subsequent generations.

The above research and theories prove that what we call consciousness in the biological sense can be inherited.

Soulless Reincarnation.

In the real world there is a purely materialistic and biological, and in accordance with and never beyond the laws of nature, process of a kind of soulless reincarnation (without the unnecessary and speculative notion of an immortal soul). This process is inheritance.

In animals such as man, for example, inheritance involves the fusion of two gametes - a male and a female - at the moment of fertilisation. Each gamete contains chromosomes, which carry genetic information. What a human being will be like is written in the DNA and this is passed on to him through the process of inheritance. And as I have shown above, man inherits not only physical characteristics, but also biological consciousness, level of intelligence, personality traits, and can also inherit mental illnesses. Thus, it can be assumed that the consciousness of previous entities is passed on in the genes to man.

Ecclesia Luciferi preaches the doctrine of a kind of godless reincarnation, or rather a soulless, materialistic transmission. It is both an anti-religious and materialistic view of biological reincarnation, according to which each entity passes on its previous life to the

next entity physically born from it. Each new entity is born perfectly godless and sinfully, naturally imperfect to live in a world completely indifferent to it.

The natural godlessness attributed to Luciferian rebellion is passed on to the next generation in the genes (man cannot reject this gift by means of free will), in an eternal cycle of birth and death. Life is eternal in this cycle as long as it is passed on, until the eternal cycle is broken, at which point eternal death occurs.

In contrast, on a more spiritual level, the concept of godless reincarnation according to the Ecclesia Luciferi is the teaching of eternal rebirth

in what Buddhists call saṃsāra, which is 'a suffering-filled, continuous cycle of life, death and rebirth, without beginning or end'.

And although the immortal soul does not exist, there is a kind of 'transfer' of the godless or sinful and soulless consciousness in the process of inheritance. In this way, a kind of immortality is possible until the eternal cycle is broken. Then eternal death occurs.

In my book The Satanic Kerygma, I write on this subject as follows:

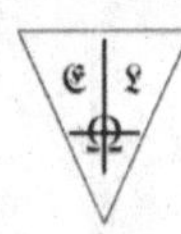

„The Satanist, who identifies with the eternal cycle of death and rebirth of the sinful nature, sees death as a transition to its eternity.

Death ends the opportunity for abundant life and the chance to consciously accept or reject the ungodly gifts of the fallen nature. Every human being receives immediately after death the gift of eternity in nothingness or the gift of the eternity of the cycle of the mortal nature, an ungodly life handed down for inheritance to the next generation, an ungodly reincarnation whose final end will take place with the end of the cycle of life itself.

To accept life in the eternal cycle of the sinful nature means to accept the Luciferian order of things. Satanists live abundantly because they have grasped what the Luciferian order of the eternal universe really is, they find their true identity in it.

To live is to embrace Lucifer's sin; where there is sin, there is life abundant and the kingdom of godlessness .

Lucifer has shown us sinful freedom through his rebellion.

The life of the ungodly consists in the full possession of the fruits of flesh and blood by Satanic self-consciousness, which includes in its ungodly glory those who have discovered it and identified themselves

with its will. Earthly pleasures are available to those perfectly united with the Luciferian consciousness of the natural world.

The ecstasy of the instincts in those perfectly united with the Luciferian order of nature sometimes exceeds the possibilities of conscious understanding and imagination. This must be experienced.

Ecclesia Luciferi's more important books:

Biblia Satanae

Biblia Satanae is the primary book using the method of doubt - the mystery of godlessness.

It is a tool for anti-theistic disenchantment.

An understanding of the method used in it and the message of this book can be applied with equal force to any 'revealed' book, not just the Judeo-Christian Bible.

Missale Satanae

Missale Satanae contains a description of satanic rites such as the satanic mass and exorcism.

Extrema Unctio: Satanic Last Rites

The book Extrema Unctio contains a satanic ritualistic text on dying.

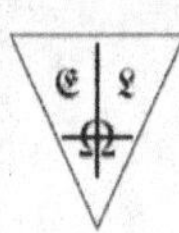

It is intended for the dying, for the already dead, but also for those who experience death during their lifetime.

The text describes real human agony, but also the experience of the death of spiritual delusions and the rise to life in the glory of flesh and blood.

Extrema Unctio is a satanic book of passage, a ritual of the last anointing before ascending into the luciferic light, into the realm of undifferentiation.